Intermediate
Moo Duk Kwan
TAE KWON DO
Korean Art of Self-Defense
Volume 2

by Richard Chun, Ph. D
Associate Professor
Hunter College, City University of New York

Editor: Gregory Lee
Graphic Design: Karen Massad

Art Production: Mary Schepis

© 1983 Copyright by R. Chun
All rights reserved
Printed in the United States of America
Library of Congress Catalog Card No.: 81-186107
ISBN: 0-89750-085-7

Eighth printing 1998

WARNING

OHARA █ PUBLICATIONS, INCORPORATED
SANTA CLARITA, CALIFORNIA

Dr. Un Yong Kim

DEDICATION

To the Honorable Dr. Un Yong Kim, President of The World Taekwondo Federation, the Korea Taekwondo Association, Kuk Ki Won, and the Executive Member of International Olympic Committee;

And also to the Presidents of Moo Duk Kwan and Moo Duk Hoi:
Master Hwang Kee—1st President
Master Kang Ik Lee—2nd President
Master Chong Soo Hong—3rd President
Master In Seok Kim—4th President
Master Nam Do Choi—5th President
Master Chong Soo Hong—1st President of Moo Duk Hoi

PREFACE

In recognition of the great devotion and many long hours that you have contributed to furthering the art of tae kwon do, I must congratulate you upon your most recent achievement—the completion of your second moo duk kwan book. It is a pleasure to see that your tireless efforts and energies have culminated in a much needed guide for the advanced student of moo duk hoi that is of the same excellent quality found in your first book.

As you will realize, it is exceedingly difficult to capture in words and express the true essence and philosophy of tae kwon do. Yet, these intangibles are as much a part of tae kwon do as the perfection of physical expertise. It is gratifying to find that in your book you have tried to convey to the students that as they enter a more advanced study of art, their progression and mastery of physical techniques must be accompanied with an awareness of the meaning of the art and an acceptance of its consequent responsibilities. Despite the difficulties found in communicating these aspects of tae kwon do and moo duk kwan, it is of vital importance that these integral parts of the study of moo duk kwan are not neglected while transmitting the art to Western culture.

My great hope, which I am sure is in accord with your own motivations and concentration of efforts in moo duk kwan, is that the furtherance of the art will result in a greater mutual respect, not only between the cultures of East and West, but on the personal level as well between teachers, students and their environment. The study of tae kwon do not only teaches one that he must learn patience to understand and cope with human weaknesses and frailties, but more importantly, teaches him to recognize the potential for human growth, development and achievement.

I am confident that your second book on moo duk kwan will not only benefit the members of Moo Duk Hoi, but also all practitioners of tae kwon do and other martial arts. I would again like to congratulate you upon the completion of your second book and I hope that you will continue your work in advancing and promoting the art.

Chong Soo Hong
President
Moo Duk Hoi
Seoul, Korea

ABOUT THE AUTHOR

Richard Chun, one of the highest-ranking instructors in tae kwon do in the world, received his ninth dan from the Kuk Ki Won /World Taekwondo Federation. His many impressive credentials include his appointment to the technical committee of the World Taekwondo Federation in 1980, and being named Special Assistant to the President of WTF. He is currently President of the United States Taekwondo Association.

Richard Chun began studying tae kwon do at an early age under Chong Soo Hong in Seoul, Korea, and with Ki Whang Kim. He graduated from Yon Sei University in 1957, where he served as the Team Captain to the Taekwondo Club. He came to the United States in 1962 in order to attend graduate school at the Long Island University in New York. Two years later, he received his M.B.A. degree in Marketing from the School of Business Administration, and his Ph.D. in Education in 1983.

In 1972, Richard Chun was appointed International Master Instructor by the World Taekwondo Federation. Since then he has worked continuously to promote the art and the sport of tae kwon do throughout the world. Chun was head coach for the U.S. team at the First World Taekwondo Championships held in Seoul in 1973, in which the U.S. team took second place. He also served as Technical Director for the Second and the Third World Taekwondo Champion-ships, and in 1979 he was named Instuctor of the Year to *Black Belt* Magazine's Hall of Fame. In addition, he was appointed as an international referee by the World Taekwondo Federation.

Richard Chun has written many articles and features about tae kwon do for various publications, including the books, *Tae Kwon Do—Korean Martial Art,* and *Advancing in Tae Kwon Do*. He has also produced a number of instructional videotapes on the same subject, including *Self-Defense for Women—Fight Back.*

Master Chun maintains his central headquarters in New York City, and has supervised much of the instruction of his art in the United States since 1962.

Dr. Richard Chun is currently an Associate Professor of Physical Education at Hunter College, City University of New York.

Dr. Richard Chun has also been very active in community service to help make his community a better place to live. He has served the New York Jay Cees as Vice-President and as the District Governor of the Lions Club International Association, and the Lions Club's New York District. For his outstanding humanitarian achievements, he has received the highest awards from the Lions Clubs International, and the Presidential Award and medal from the President of Korea.

FOREWORD

Tae Kwon Do teaches the student patience, discipline and humility. Very often a great deal of repetition is required as the student must continue to practice and improve his basic techniques as well as devote a great deal of time and effort to master new techniques. Thus, much patience and self-sacrifice is demanded of him to progress in the art.

By studying and mastering the art, the student begins to understand himself and is able to recognize both his achievements and abilities. In this stage he begins to develop the traits that will make him a leader among fellow practitioners. As he develops a clearer perception and better judgment of both himself and his opponents, he gains the confidence and self-control which enable him to remain silent and fearless when confronted with an aggressor. He can then display not only his strength, but humility, kindness and forgiveness toward his opponent.

The World Taekwondo Federation was founded in 1973 for the purpose of promoting and governing the growth of tae kwon do as both an art and a world sport. Moo Duk Kwan, as a member of the Korea Taekwondo Association, actively participated in advancing and furthering the goals of the World Taekwondo Federation.

In 1975, tae kwon do was accepted as a member of the General Assembly of International Sports Federations (GAISF) as the first step toward becoming an Olympic sport.

In July 1980, the International Olympic Committee (IOC) recognized the World Taekwondo Federation at the 83rd IOC Session meeting in Moscow and granted tae kwon do membership in Olympic Games.

In May 1981, the IOC approved the inculsion of tae kwon do in the 1988 Olympic games to be held in Korea.

In May 1982, for the purpose of helping promote tae kwon do as a martial art and sport, and also promote the friendship between the members of Moo Duk Kwan, senior ranking masters of Moo Duk Kwan formed a club named Moo Duk Hoi and elected Master Chong Soo Hong as its first president.

Due to this increasing popularity of tae kwon do and the growing number of moo duk kwan schools in the United States, many of these practitioners have urged that more books on moo duk kwan be made available. I have received a great deal of correspondence from students of the martial arts telling me of their achievements and thanking me for the instruction they have obtained from my first moo duk kwan book. I want to express my deepest hopes that these students will find guidance in this book toward learning the more advanced levels of the art of tae kwon do and the principles of moo duk kwan. I would like to take this opportunity to express my sincerest gratitude to all my students who have enabled me to make this book possible. Marco A. Vega and Margaret Sauers for their photography, and Geraldine Michalik for her editing.

Richard Chun
New York City
1982

CONTENTS

KOREAN FLAG

The flag of *tae kook* is the Korean flag. Tae kook means "the origin of all things in the universe." The circle in the center of the flag is divided into portions of red and blue by a horizontal "S." These red and blue portions symbolize the *um* and *yang* (yin and yang) theory of eternal duality which exists within nature (e.g., heaven and earth; light and darkness; hot and cold; being and not being). In science, this theory can be represented with the symbols " + " and " − ". These dualities exist as a principle of the universe.

The four *gye* (bar designs) in the corners of the flag are based on the um and yang principle of light and darkness. The location of these gye represent the four points of the compass. Ee-gye in the lower left corner, indicates dawn and early sunlight as the sun rises in the East. Kun-gye, in the upper left, represents bright sunshine when the sun is in the South. Kam-gye in the upper right corner symbolizes twilight as the sun moves to the West. Kon-gye in the lower right, indicates total darkness when the sun is in the North. Together these symbols express the mysteries of the universe.

MOO DUK KWAN EMBLEM

1. Laurel leaves—The 14 laurel leaves on each side, represent the 14 states of Korea and the advancement of peace.
2. The three seeds joined to the laurel leaves on each side of the emblem represent the "three thousand li" (the distance running north to south) of the "Land of Morning Calm" and its success.
3. The six seeds in total indicate the world and represent the six continents.
4. The fist represents tae kwon do and justice.
5. The Korean character in the center of the circle means moo duk kwan.
6. The character on the left of the circle means tae and the character on the right of the circle means kwon.
7. The deep blue color of the emblem represents the three oceans and black belts.

As a whole, the emblem symbolizes the spreading of moo duk kwan throughout the 14 states, i.e., all of Korea, and then across the oceans to the six continents of the world. Moo Duk Kwan, as an international institution, is to achieve the objectives of peace and human advancement as the emblem symbolizes.

ASPECTS OF MOO DUK KWAN

MOO DUK KWAN PRINCIPLES

1. Responsibility
2. Sincerity
3. Justice

TEN CREEDS OF MOO DUK KWAN

1. Be loyal to your country.
2. Be obedient to your parents.
3. Be loveable between husband and wife.
4. Be cooperative between brothers.
5. Be respectful to your elders.
6. Be faithful between teacher and student.
7. Be faithful between friends.
8. Be just in killing.
9. Never retreat in battle.
10. Accompany your decisions with action and always finish what you start.

ELEVEN POINTS OF EMPHASIS ON MENTAL TRAINING

1. Reverence for nature.
2. Physical concentration (Ki-up).
3. Courtesy.
4. Modesty.
5. Thankfulness.
6. Self-sacrifice.
7. Cultivate courage.
8. Chastity.
9. Be strong inside and mild outside.
10. Endurance.
11. Reading ability.

TEN POINTS OF EMPHASIS ON PHYSICAL DEVELOPMENT

1. Vocal exhalation, for thoractic strength (Ki-up).
2. Focus of sight.
3. Continuous balance during movements.
4. Flexibility of the body.
5. Correct muscle tone for maximum power.
6. High and low speed techniques.
7. Exactness of techniques.
8. Adjustment for proper distance.
9. Proper breathing for endurance.
10. Conditioning hands and feet.

FIVE REQUISITES ON MENTAL TRAINING

1. Oneness with nature.
2. Complete awareness of environment.
3. Experience.
4. Conscience.
5. Culture.

MATTERS THAT DEMAND SPECIAL ATTENTION WHILE TRAINING IN MOO DUK KWAN

1. Purpose of training should be enhancement of the mental and physical self.
2. Sincerity is necessary.
3. Effort is necessary.
4. Consistent schedule during practice.
5. Do your best when training.
6. Train in the basic spirit of moo duk kwan.
7. Regularly spaced practice sessions.
8. Obey without objection the word of instructors or seniors; look and learn.
9. Don't be overly ambitious.
10. Pay attention to every aspect of your training.
11. Pay attention to the order of training.
12. Get instruction step by step in new forms and techniques.
13. Try to conquer when you feel idleness.
14. Cleanliness is desired after practice is finished.

GUIDANCE POLICY
OF THE PRESIDENT
OF MOO DUK KWAN

1. Protect the art of tae kwon do with justice.
2. Cultivate character and personality through training for discipline.
3. Unity through sincerity and courtesy.

BOWING PROCEDURE

The first thing a beginning student must learn is how to bow, which is the Oriental way of showing respect. The practitioner of tae kwon do bows to the training area, to the flags on the wall, to the instructor at the beginning and end of class, and to a partner before and after sparring.

How to Bow

The student stands at attention in a ready stance (either with heels touching and toes pointing at a 45-degree angle to the outside in a V-shape or with both feet parallel and shoulder width apart). Hands may be either held open at the side of the body, or in a fist in front of the body.

Bend at the waist to about a 45-degree angle. Eyes look downward, except in sparring when eyes are kept on the lower part of the opponent's body.

UNIFORM AND BELT SYSTEM IN MOO DUK KWAN

The *to bok* (uniform) with trim is the traditional moo duk kwan uniform. Black belt holders of moo duk kwan wear black trimmed uniforms in most countries. However, in Korea, the Taekwondo Association regulates that all its members, including members of Moo Duk Kwan, wear a solid white uniform. Eventually, the World Taekwondo Federation will recommend that its members also wear the white uniform.

BELT SYSTEM

Rank	Color
Black belts	Black
1st-3rd kup	Red
4th-6th kup	Green
7th-8th kup	Yellow
9th and under (no kup)	White

The belt system described above is the official system of Moo Duk Kwan in Korea. However, in the U.S. the belt system varies from school to school as an incentive for its students.

TAE KWON DO AS A SPORT

In recent years, tae kwon do has spread rapidly in popularity as a competitive sport throughout the world. The World Taekwondo Federation has played an important role in training qualified referees and in developing rules and regulations for championship tournaments to help and encourage the spread of tae kwon do as a sport. The World Taekwondo Federation has held two World Championships, in 1973 and 1975. The Federation has also held three International Referee Seminars in 1974, 1975 and 1976. It has also conducted the Asia Taekwondo Championship and the European Taekwondo Championship in 1975 and 1976.

In October, 1975, tae kwon do was officially accepted as a new member by the General Assembly of International Sports Federations (GAISF). This was the first step toward becoming an international sport which can qualify as an event in the Olympic Games.

In championship tournaments, contestants wear chest protectors, head gear, cup supporters and shin guards to allow full contact by both foot and hand techniques. Full contact to the face is permitted only with foot techniques. Official rules and regulations for scoring points have been published by the World Taekwondo Federation. There are many local tournaments which are open to all styles of the martial arts and therefore, the regulations are often modified to suit the particular tournament.

With the great efforts of Dr. Un Yong Kim, IOC member and the President of WTF, tae kwon do was included as a member of the Olympic sports. Tae kwon do was included in the 1988 Seoul Olympic Games as a demonstration game and again will be included in 1992 Olympic Games to be held in Spain. It may participate in the 1996 Olympics as an official game.

STRIKING WEAPONS
AND TARGET AREAS

Basic striking weapons such as the forefist, forearms, elbow, knife-hand, spear-hand, ball of the foot, bottom of the heel and instep should be reviewed and studied from Volume I before learning the advanced striking weapons described in this chapter. The drawing of the vital target areas shown in Volume I should also be reviewed in order to obtain the maximum results from aiming and attacking the vital target areas correctly.

This chapter covers advanced striking weapons such as the back fist, middle finger one knuckle fist, four knuckle fist, tiger mouth hand, ridge hand, palm heel, back hand, wrist, arch of the foot, knee, and head.

Application of the more advanced tae kwon do techniques requires that the student develop and condition certain portions of the body which can become deadly striking weapons. The pattern of attack and defense must vary according to each situation. Thus, it is important to develop maximum power and speed in numerous portions of the body which can be chosen as the most appropriate and effective striking weapons for the given situation.

BACK FIST

Clench your hand the same as in making a forefist. The striking surface is the back of the second knuckle. This is effective in strikes to the face and temple.

ONE KNUCKLE FIST

Clench your hand as if to make a forefist, then extend the middle knuckle of your middle finger forward to make a striking point. This is effective in strikes to the temple, below the nose and to the ribs.

HAMMER FIST

Clench your hand the same as in making a forefist. The striking surface is the bottom of the fist. This is effective in strikes to the head, the side of the face, and the collarbone.

FOUR-KNUCKLE FIST

The striking area is formed by the middle knuckles of all your fingers extended from a forefist. This is effective in strikes to the bridge of the nose, below the nose and the throat.

RIDGE HAND

Extend your four fingers straight forward as in a knife hand with your thumb tucked into your palm. The striking surface is the outer edge of the first knuckle (the palm is usually turned down, however a strike can also be delivered palm up). This is effective in strikes to the temple, face, neck and throat.

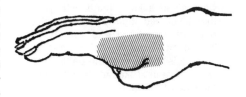

TIGER MOUTH HAND

Tense your four fingers, curved slightly inward, palm down, with your thumb extending forward, also tensed and curved. The striking surface is the curve between the thumb and the forefinger. This is effective in strikes to the throat.

WRIST

Arch and tense your wrist with your open fingers curved inward. The striking surface is the back of the wrist. This is effective in strikes to the face and the stomach.

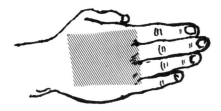

BACK HAND

Extend your four fingers straight forward as in a knife hand with your thumb curved inward and closed under the ridge of your hand. The striking surface is the back of your hand. This is effective in strikes to the face and the ears.

PALM HEEL

Extend your four fingers straight forward as in a knife hand with your thumb curved tightly against the ridge of your hand and your hand bent back at the wrist. The striking surface is the heel of the palm. This is effective in strikes to the chin and the side of the face.

ARCH OF THE FOOT

The arch is tensed with your toes pulled up. The striking surface is the arch of the foot. This is effective in strikes to the face, arms and legs.

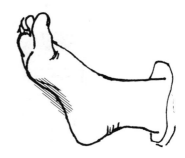

KNEE

The knee is an effective weapon in close combat and can be used in strikes to the face, abdomen, stomach and groin.

HEAD

The head is an effective weapon in close combat and can be used in strikes to the face. (The forehead, side of the head and back of the head can be used as a striking weapon.)

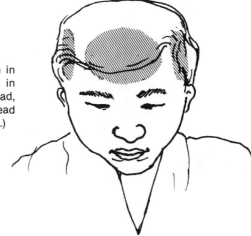

VITAL TARGET AREAS

(FRONT)

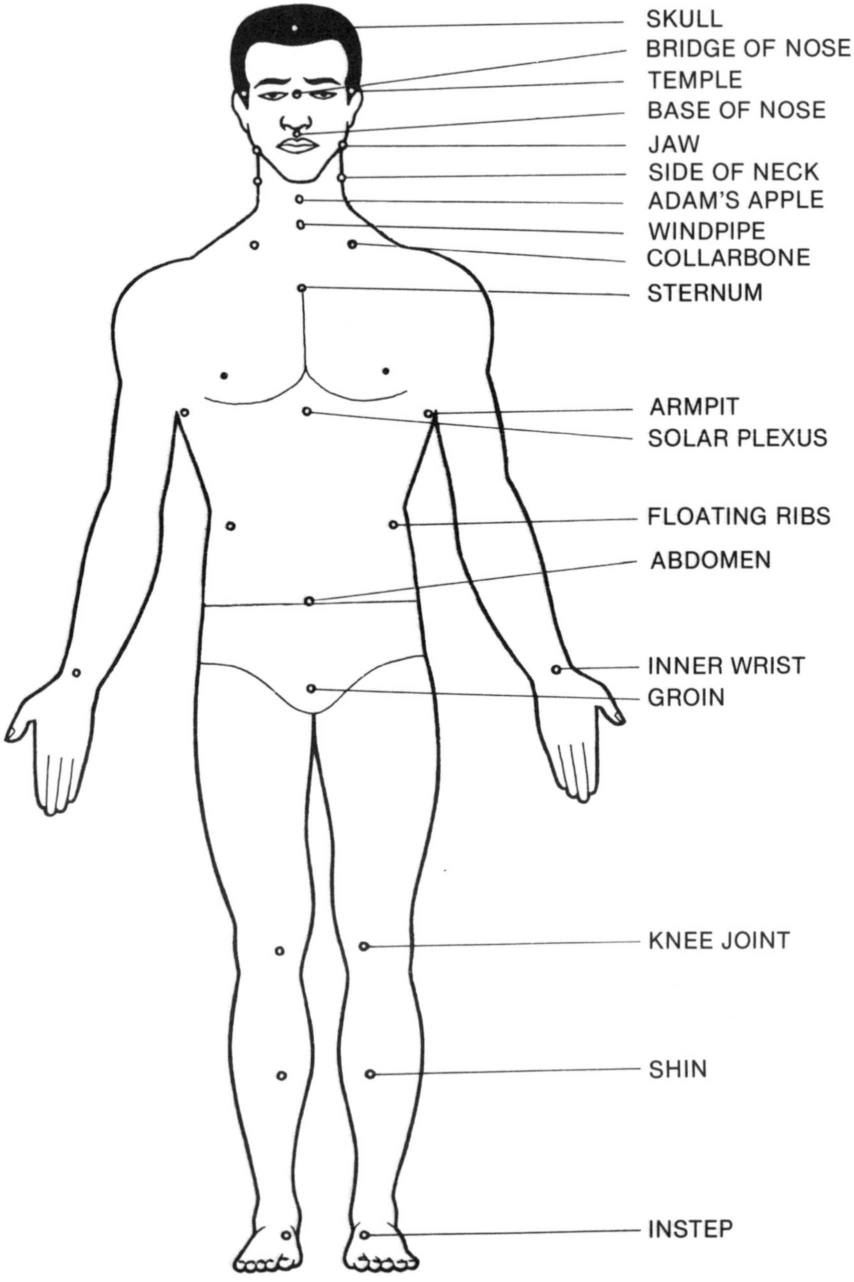

- SKULL
- BRIDGE OF NOSE
- TEMPLE
- BASE OF NOSE
- JAW
- SIDE OF NECK
- ADAM'S APPLE
- WINDPIPE
- COLLARBONE
- STERNUM

- ARMPIT
- SOLAR PLEXUS

- FLOATING RIBS
- ABDOMEN

- INNER WRIST
- GROIN

- KNEE JOINT

- SHIN

- INSTEP

VITAL TARGET AREAS

(BACK)

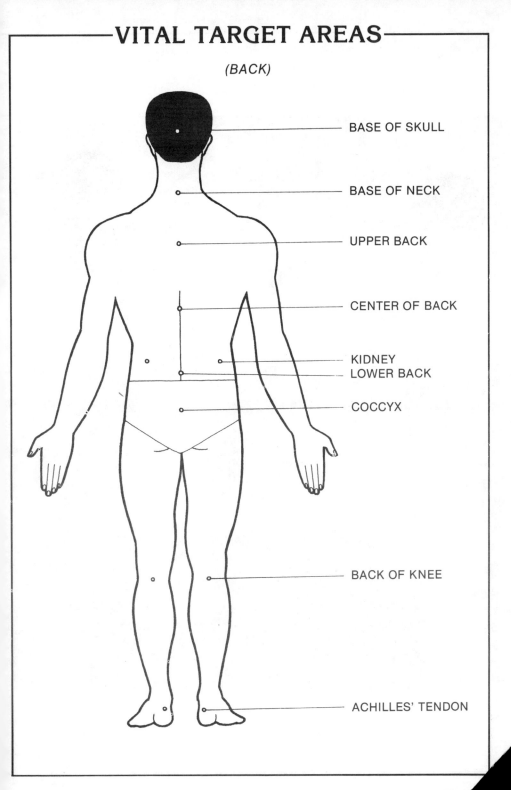

BASE OF SKULL

BASE OF NECK

UPPER BACK

CENTER OF BACK

KIDNEY
LOWER BACK

COCCYX

BACK OF KNEE

ACHILLES' TENDON

WARM-UP EXERCISES

To practice advanced tae kwon do techniques correctly, certain muscles of the body must be kept more limber than in basic training. Thus a more intensive and longer warm-up period is needed to loosen and relax the body in order to perform more advanced movements without injury. A proper routine of warm-up exercises is necessary to relax the mind, establish a sense of confidence and develop the flexability and control needed to prepare the body for execution of more strenuous techniques. It is also important to remember that the body needs to be refreshed with correct breathing from time to time by inhaling deeply through the nose and exhaling completely through the mouth.

The best warm-up exercise for conditioning the body, limbering the muscles and building stamina is jogging. It is recommended that the student establish a daily exercise routine which includes a few miles of jogging.

The side stretch, leg stretch, push-ups, side splits, front kick stretch and side kick stretch, which were covered in Volume I, should already be a part of your daily exercise routine. In addition, you should now practice the exercises described in this chapter.

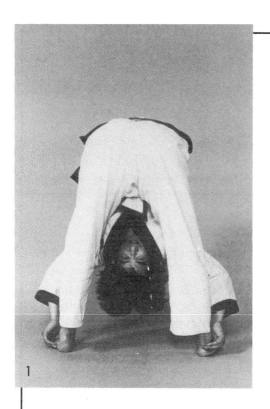

1

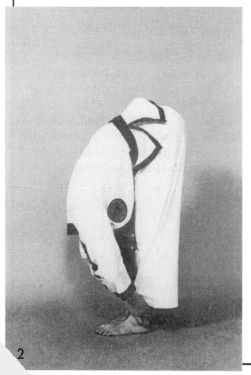

2

FORWARD AND BACKWARD BENDS

(1&2) Spread your feet slightly wider than shoulder width apart. Then bend forward from the waist until you can touch the floor with your fingertips. Do this exercise five times gradually, then bend deeper until you can touch your palms to the floor. Now bend all the way, grabbing your ankles with

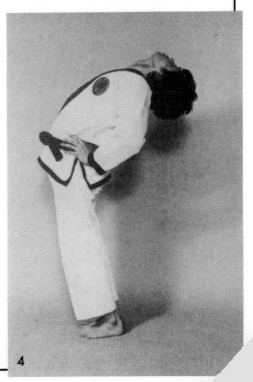

3

your hands, and touch your head to your knees. Now place your hands on your hips (3&4) and bend your body backward as far as you can. Repeat this exercise five times, then practice both forward and backward bends while keeping the feet together.

4

HAND AND LEG STRETCH

(1) Balance on one leg while lifting your opposite knee as high as possible. Keep the instep and toes of your raised foot tensed and pointing downward. Simultaneously stretch both arms over your head and push upward with the palms of your hand. Switch feet. (2) Balance on one leg while grabbing your opposite foot with the same hand. Pull your leg upward behind your body while stretching your opposite arm forward. Switch to the opposite leg and repeat.

LEG AND BACK STRETCH

Begin in a sitting position with one leg stretched out in front of you and the other leg bent behind and to the side. Slowly bend your body backward until you are lying completely flat on the floor.

LEG STRETCH

(1) Face a partner and rest your leg on your partner's opposite shoulder. Keep your body erect and your knees locked, stretching your leg completely. Hold for five seconds. (2) Pull the toes and instep of your raised foot downward, then turn your leg slightly inward. Keep your knees locked to stretch the side muscles of your leg

2

completely. Hold for five seconds. (3) Now turn your body in the opposite direction while turning your foot and ankle completely inward. Keep your knees locked and stretch the back muscles of your leg and the muscles of your lower back. Hold. Repeat these three stretches with your other leg.

3

SITTING FRONT STRETCH I

From a sitting position (1&2) grasp the heel of your right foot with your right hand and pull the leg up toward your body as high as possible with your knee locked. The opposite leg on the floor is extended. Now repeat (2) with the left leg, grasping the heel with the left hand.

SITTING FRONT STRETCH II

(1) With one leg stretched straight out in front of you, grab the heel of your opposite foot with both hands and pull your leg upward, behind your head if possible. Now repeat with the other leg. (2) Repeat this exercise for both legs with your front foot bent inward to your opposite thigh.

SITTING FRONT STRETCH III

(1) With one leg stretched straight in front of you, bring the opposite foot on top of your thigh as close to your waist as possible. While maintaining this position, bend forward (2) until your forehead touches your knees. Repeat this exercise about ten times for both legs.

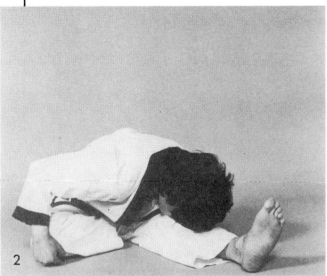

FRONT SPLIT

(1) Keeping your body erect, stretch one leg in front and one leg behind you. Keep bouncing gently until your legs stretch out completely. (2) From this position, bend forward until your forehead touches your knees. Now reverse the legs and repeat.

WRIST EXERCISE

(1) Extend your arms forward with elbows slightly bent, placing one hand inside and one hand outside that of your partner's. Tighten your wrists, while pushing

against your partner's wrists, and move your hands (2-6) in a circular motion counterclockwise. Now move clockwise, with your partner offering resistance.

STANCES

This chapter covers advanced stances such as the normal stance, V-stance, high front stance, cat stance, crane stance, and the front, forward and backward side cross stances.

In order for the advanced student to develop maximum speed, power and accuracy, it is important to maintain perfectly balanced stances. It is especially important in free sparring to develop a balanced stance for maneuverability in attacking and blocking effectively against an opponent according to his size and distance.

Basic stances such as the ready stance, horseback stance, front stance, back stance, and walking and turning with these stances should be reviewed and studied from Volume I before learning the advanced stances described in this chapter.

NORMAL STANCE

Stand with your feet together, toes pointed straight forward and knees locked. Place your open hands near your thighs, palm in and fingers pointed downward.

V-STANCE

This is identical to the normal stance except that you stand with your heels together and your toes point outward at about a 45-degree angle.

HIGH FRONT STANCE

Assume a position similar to the front stance (Volume I, p. 36) with your feet shoulder width apart and toes pointed slightly outward. The distance from your back heel to your front heel should be about one step. The front knee is slightly bent, with two-thirds of your weight on the front foot.

CAT STANCE

The distance between your front foot and back foot is about one-half step. The ball of your front foot touches the floor with the heel raised about one fist high, toes pointing straight forward and the knee bent over your toes. Place 100 percent of your weight on your back foot, toes pointing outward at a right angle and knee bent over your toes.

CRANE STANCE

The crane stance is used in most cases to prepare for a side kick or a back kick. Stand with 100 percent of your weight on one foot, knee slightly bent and toes pointed forward. Raise your other foot, toes pointed forward near the knee of your supporting leg.

FRONT CROSS STANCE

Stand with 90 percent of your weight on your front foot (supporting leg), toes pointed forward. Cross your back foot behind your front foot with the instep resting against the heel of your front foot and the ball of your back foot touching the floor. Your front knee is bent forward over your toes and the back knee is bent outward.

FORWARD
SIDE CROSS STANCE

This stance is usually used for preparing to execute a side kick. Stand with 90 percent of your weight on your back foot (supporting leg), toes pointing forward and knee slightly bent. Slide your other foot sideways, toes pointing forward, crossing in front of your supporting leg with only the ball of your foot touching the floor and knee slightly bent.

BACKWARD
SIDE CROSS STANCE

This stance is usually used for preparing to execute a back kick. Stand with 90 percent of your weight on your front foot (supporting leg), toes pointing forward and knee slightly bent. Slide your other foot sideways, toes pointing forward, crossing your foot behind your supporting leg with the ball of your back foot touching the floor and knee slightly bent.

PUNCHING AND STRIKING TECHNIQUES

Basic punching techniques such as the straight punch, reverse punch, side punch, walking and turning with these punches and their respective applications should be reviewed and studied from Volume I before learning the advanced punching techniques described in this chapter.

This chapter covers advanced punching techniques such as the uppercut punch, double uppercut punch, round punch, hook punch, back fist strike, one knuckle fist punch, four knuckle fist punch, tiger mouth thrust, ridge hand strike, palm heel thrust, back hand strike, wrist strike, and head strike.

In order for these techniques to be completely effective, it is important to practice them correctly and to develop speed and accuracy while mastering them. To develop an effective attack the advanced student must learn to use a variety of punching and striking techniques depending upon the opponent's size, height and proximity.

UPPERCUT PUNCH

(1) Draw your fist back, palm down, near your ribs. Then snap your arm forward and up (2&3), twisting your wrist, palm up. This is an effective short range attack (4) for strik-

ing the chin or solar plexus. (4A) The double uppercut punch is applied in the same manner by using both hands simultaneously for the same purpose.

HOOK PUNCH

(1) Draw your fist back, palm up, at waist level. Then move your fist forward (2&3) across your chest with your elbow

bent sharply inward, striking palm down. This is an effective attack (4) for striking the chin, solar plexus, temple and jaw.

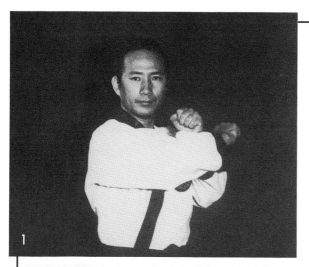

BACK FIST STRIKE

(1) Place the fist of your striking hand in front of the opposite shoulder at chin level, palm down, your elbow bent. Twist (2&3) your wrist palm up as you snap your fist forward. The striking surface is the first two

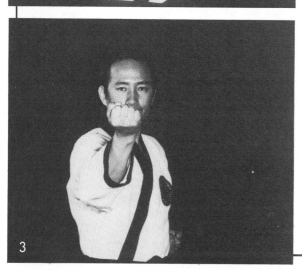

knuckles of your fist. This is an effective close-range attack (4) to the face area or solar plexus. (4A) The side back fist strike is delivered in the same manner by snapping the fist sideways to the side of the opponent's head.

HAMMER FIST STRIKE

(1) Place the fist of your striking hand in front of the opposite shoulder at chin level, palm in, your elbow bent. Twist your wrist palm out (2&3), raising your arm up and out to strike downward like a hammer. The strik-

ing surface is the bottom of the fist. This is an effective strike (4) to the face or top of the head. The hammer fist can also be delivered to the side by moving your arm out in an arc, sideways, striking with the palm down.

ONE KNUCKLE PUNCH

This punch can be executed in the same manner as the straight punch for a long distance strike to the face area; as a hook punch, palm up, for a close attack to the ribs, solar plexus or neck; as a round punch to strike the temple; and as a single or double hand horizontal strike to the ribs and temple.

FOUR KNUCKLE PUNCH

This punch is used in the same manner as the one knuckle fist punch, but employs all four knuckles.

TIGER MOUTH THRUST

Tense your fingers into the tiger mouth, palm down, and thrust forward in a punching manner to attack the opponent's throat and neck.

RIDGE HAND STRIKE

Tense your fingers into the ridge hand, palm down, and snap a strike in an arc from outside to inside at the opponent's temple, face or throat.

PALM HEEL THRUST

Tense your hand into a palm heel, and thrust forward, palm up, in a punching manner to strike the opponent's chin, ribs or solar plexus.

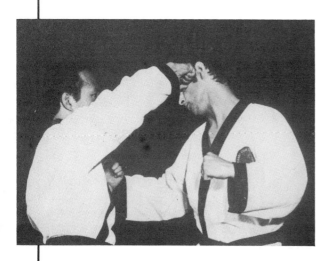

ROUND PUNCH

Draw your fist back, palm up, at waist level. Then move your fist forward in a slight arc inward, striking palm down with your elbow slightly bent. This is an effective attack to the jaw or temple.

BACK HAND STRIKE

Tense your fingers, palm open, and snap forward from the opposite shoulder, striking the opponent's face or ribs with the back knuckles. This strike can be used to attack an opponent in front of you or to the side.

WRIST STRIKE

Arch and tense your wrist, palm down and in, with the fingers curled under. Snap your wrist forward to strike the opponent's face, neck, ribs, stomach or groin.

HEAD STRIKE

The top of your forehead can be used to strike an opponent's face by seizing the temples of the opponent between your hands and snapping your head sharply forward.

BLOCKING TECHNIQUES

Basic blocking techniques such as the low block, high block, inside middle block, outside middle block, knife hand block variations, walking and turning with these blocks and their respective applications should be reviewed and studied from Volume I before learning the advanced blocking techniques covered in this chapter.

This chapter covers advanced blocking techniques such as the double hand blocks (high and middle), double hand low block variation, spread blocks (inner edge of forearm, outer edge of forearm and spread knife hand block), scissor block, X-block (low, high and knife hand high), palm heel (downward, upward and sideward), double hand high and middle block, double hand lifting middle block, back hand block, knee block, front kick block, side kick block and crescent kick block.

Since the primary purpose of tae kwon do as a martial art is self-defense, it is especially important to learn and develop advanced blocking techniques. An effectively applied block can be used not only for defensive purposes but also serves as a preliminary counterattack when it is used to break the opponent's balance.

DOUBLE HAND BLOCKS

The double hand block can be applied as a high, middle or low block and is used with either a front or back stance. This block is stronger than a single hand block, since the assisting hand reinforces the blocking hand and arm, protects the midsection and is prepared for a counterattack. The blocking surface is the inner edge of the forearm.

DOUBLE HAND MIDDLE BLOCK

(1) Your blocking arm is drawn across your chest with your forearm parallel to the floor and your fist near the opposite shoulder, palm down. The opposite hand is placed, palm down, at waist level, and your elbow drawn back. (2) Pull your blocking hand forward in front of your chest while twisting the wrist palm in. Move your other hand forward, twisting your wrist palm up. (3) Your blocking hand

2

passes all the way to the front of your body, stopping directly in front of your shoulder (your fist at shoulder level). Your arm is bent at an angle of 120 degrees. The wrist of your other hand is completely palm up, placed horizontally in front of your stomach and against your blocking arm.
Application: Against a punch to the midsection.

APPLICATION

3

65

DOUBLE HAND HIGH BLOCK

(1&2) A double hand high block is executed in the same manner as a double hand middle block except that the blocking hand sweeps upward to block at forehead level. The other hand is placed across the chest, palm up.
Application: Against a face punch.

APPLICATION

WALKING DOUBLE HAND MIDDLE BLOCK

(1) Assume a ready stance. (2) While stepping forward with your left foot bring both hands to your right side, palm down, left fist above the right fist at shoulder level. (3) Pull both hands forward in front of your chest executing the block in the left front stance. (4&5) Step forward with the right foot while simultaneously drawing the fists back, palm down, with the right fist above the left. (6) Execute a middle block as you enter the right front stance. Practice moving both backward and forward alternately, executing the steps and blocks simultaneously. Also practice the double hand high blocks in the same manner.

1

4

2

3

5

6

1

TURNING WITH DOUBLE HAND MIDDLE BLOCK

(1) To turn from a left front stance (or left back stance) while executing a double hand middle block, pivot (2) on both feet while bringing both hands to your left side, palms down, with

2

your right fist at shoulder height over your left. (3&4) Step into the right front (or right back) stance, simultaneously executing the block to the right.

DOUBLE HAND
LOW BLOCK

(1-3) This block is executed in the same manner as the double hand block except that the blocking hand begins near the opposite shoulder, palm in, and the other hand at waist level, palm down. The block is com-

2

pleted with the blocking hand extended palm down over the front knee and the other hand placed in front of the stomach, palm up.

Application: Against a front snap kick.

APPLICATION

3

SPREAD BLOCKS

The spread block is effective in defending against a two-handed choke or when an attacker grabs your lapels or head.

SPREAD BLOCK
(Inner Edge of Forearm)

(1) From a ready position, draw your fists up to shoulder level, crossing your wrists (2) in front of your chest with palms facing out. (3) Simultaneously snap both arms outward to the

side, twisting your wrists palm in and blocking with the inner edge of each forearm.
Application: Against a two hand grab.

APPLICATION

SPREAD BLOCK
(Outer Edge of Forearm)

(1) From a ready position, draw your fists up to shoulder level, crossing your wrists in front of your chest (2) with the palms facing in. (3) Simultaneously snap both arms outward to

the side, twisting your wrists palm out and blocking with the outer edge of each forearm.

Application: Against a two hand grab.

APPLICATION

SPREAD BLOCK
(Knife Hand)

This block is executed like the spread block using the outer edge of the forearm, but the hands are held in the knife hand position, palms up at the waist. (1) From a ready position, draw your hands up to shoulder level (2) crossing the wrists in front of your

2

chest with palms facing in. (3) Simultaneously snap both arms outward to the side, twisting your wrists palm out and blocking with the outer edges of each knife hand.

Application: Against two hand grabs.

APPLICATION

3

SCISSORS BLOCK

This block is for defending against a simultaneous attack to both the high and lower portions of the body. (1) Hold your right arm across your chest at chin level, your right fist just in front of your opposite shoulder. Your left arm is across your lower abdomen, left fist at waist level. (2) Cross both forearms in front of the chest

2

and begin to twist the right fist palm down and the left fist palm in. (3) Snap the arms out simultaneously, the right arm blocking low with the outer edge of the forearm, and the left arm blocking high with the inner edge of the forearm.

Application: Counters simultaneously a low kick and a high punch.

APPLICATION

3

X-BLOCK

The X-block is an effective defense against a kick since both arms reinforce each other, affording the groin and abdomen greater protection. The X-block can also be a strike in itself when both fists are tightened and used to counterstrike.

LOW X-BLOCK

(1) Place both fists, right over left and palms in, at your side at rib level. (2) Simultaneously snap both fists forward and down in front of your abdomen, keeping the wrists crossed and using the X-shape formed by the back of your fists to block.
Application: Against a front kick.

APPLICATION

HIGH X-BLOCK

(1) Begin this block in the same position as the low X-block (if your arms are held on the left side, the left fist should be held over the right, or opposite of what is shown here). (2) Snap the fists forward and up in front of your head, keeping the wrists crossed and using the outer edge of the fists in the X-shape to block the attack.

Application: Against a face punch.

APPLICATION

HIGH X-BLOCK
(Knife Hand)

This block is executed in the same manner as the other X-blocks, except that the hands are tensed in the open knife hand position. (1) The hands are held to one side, the right hand over the left (if you are blocking from the right side) near the waist. (2) Snap both arms upward simultaneously, blocking with the outer edge of each knife hand in front of the head. The open knife hand X-block enables you to immediately grab your opponent's attacking arm, to twist or break the opponent's wrist, or to disarm him. *Application:* Against a face punch.

APPLICATION

PALM HEEL BLOCK

The palm heel block is a flexible and powerful block since it can be used both to defend against an attack and as a countermove to grab and throw an opponent off balance in order to prepare for a counterattack. There are three ways to execute this block: down, up and sideways. The blocking surface is the palm and heel of the hand.

PALM HEEL BLOCK
(Downward)

(1) Raise your open knife hand (in this case, the right), palm out, at shoulder level and tense the hand with your wrist bent tightly upward. The left hand remains low to protect the mid-

2

section. (2&3) Push downward sharply with the palm heel to block an attack to the midsection or groin.
Application: Against a front snap kick.

APPLICATION

3

PALM HEEL BLOCK
(Upward)

(1) Lower your open knife hand, palm down, to the side at waist level, keeping the palm heel tensed and the hand bent upward at the wrist. The other hand remains high to protect

2

the midsection. (2&3) Push upward sharply with your palm heel to block an attack.

Application: Against a face punch.

APPLICATION

3

PALM HEEL BLOCK
(Sideways)

(1) Raise your open knife hand, palm out, to shoulder level and to the side, elbow bent and wrist bent tightly upward. The other arm remains in front of the chest to block. (2) Push forward and across your chest in a sweeping arc, blocking the attack.
Application: Against a face punch.

APPLICATION

DOUBLE HAND BLOCK
(High and Middle)

This block is effective in defending against an attack from the front and side simultaneously. To block to the right side, (1) bring both fists toward your left hip with your right fist (palm in) resting over your left fist (palm up) at waist level. (2&3) Snap both arms simultaneously upward and to the

2

side, forming a right hand outside middle block and a left hand high block. Now reverse the direction of the blocks and counter to an attack from the left side. This block is executed best from a back stance.
Application: Against a forward punch and a knife hand strike to the side.

APPLICATION

3

1

DOUBLE HAND LIFTING BLOCK

(1) The blocking arm (in this example, the right one) is drawn across your chest parallel to the ground with your fist palm up. Your left fist is turned palm down at the waist beneath your right fist with the elbow drawn back. (2) Snap both arms forward with your blocking arm moving up and out and your wrist twisting palm out. Your opposite hand begins to twist palm up. (3) Your right arm is now com-

2

pletely forward in a high block, palm out. Your other arm protects your midsection and can support your blocking arm, with the palm up.

Application: This block is particularly effective against kicks aimed at the midsection. You are now in a position to raise the kicking leg of your opponent to upset his balance, and counterattack with the left hand.

APPLICATION

3

BACK HAND BLOCK

(1) The blocking arm (in this example, the right one) is drawn across your chest, the right palm open above the opposite shoulder. Your left arm is placed across the midsection below your right arm, fist turned palm down. (2&3) Snap your tensed back hand outward and level with your shoulder, blocking with the back of the hand.

2

Draw your left hand simultaneously back to your rear hip, twisting the fist palm up.

Application: This block is very useful for blocking a punch and then grabbing the opponent's arm, usually followed with a crescent kick to break the opponent's elbow.

APPLICATION

3

LEG BLOCKS

Using the leg to block a kick to your groin or midsection is an excellent defensive counter, since you are now in a position to step forward with the blocking leg and counterattack immediately. The outer knee, shin or foot all may be used to block.

KNEE BLOCK

To block a kick with the knee, raise the leg (in this case, the right leg) high and in toward your torso, protecting the front of your body. The fists should always be held high, ready to counterattack.
Application: Against a front snap kick.

APPLICATION

FRONT KICK BLOCK

This block is executed in the same manner as a front kick, using the ball of the foot as the blocking surface. *Application:* This is effective when your opponent comes too close and is applied by pushing against the opponent's leg as he is about to deliver a kick. This can also be used to block if the kick is about half or slightly less than completed.

APPLICATION

SIDE KICK BLOCK

This block is executed in the same manner as a side kick, using the outer edge of the foot as the blocking surface.

Application: This block is used for the same purpose as the front kick block, stopping a snap kick before or just after an opponent tries to launch one.

APPLICATION

CRESCENT KICK BLOCK

This block is executed in the same manner as a crescent kick, using the arch of the foot as the blocking surface.

Application: This block is used for the same purpose as the front kick block, stopping an opponent's snap kick and possibly forcing him off balance, leaving an opening for your counterattack.

APPLICATION

KICKING TECHNIQUES

This chapter covers advanced kicking techniques, such as the hop kick, hook kick, wheel kick, crescent kick, turning kicks and jumping kicks.

Tae kwon do emphasizes kicking techniques since they are more useful in combat as well as for self-defense. Due to the great amount of power generated in the maneuverability of the hip and the longer-range striking distance, the leg can be a more devastating weapon than the hand if the kick is delivered properly. Kicking techniques are more difficult to master however, and great patience and repeated practice are needed before you can apply your kicks as powerful, accurate weapons.

Most advance kicks are just variations of the basic kicks: front kick, side kick, back kick, etc. Therefore, it is important that you master these basic kicks before studying the more advanced techniques covered here. All the basic kicks and their applications (and correct hand positions) have been covered in Volume I, and should be reviewed and practiced daily to increase speed, power and accuracy, even as you learn the kicks in this chapter.

HOP KICKS

The hop kick is used to reach your opponent as rapidly as possible. The hop kick is executed by bringing the back foot forward and close to the front foot, while simultaneously raising the knee of the front foot to deliver a kick. This movement should be executed as one smooth motion. The hop kick may be applied with

ROUND HOP KICK
(Instep Kick)

(1) From a back stance, bring your back foot forward (2) close to your front foot as you lift your front foot up onto your toes, instep tensed. (3) Raise your front knee to waist level pointed forward, toes

many different kicks, but is most often used with a front, side, round, or hook kick. In most cases the hop kick is executed from either a back stance or horseback stance. The round hop kick is illustrated below as an example of how to execute a hop kick.

drawn back pointed down. (4) Lean back on your back foot and execute a swift round kick to your opponent's head. The kick should follow the hop immediately, without a pause.

HOOK KICK

The hook kick is useful in catching your opponent unaware since it can appear to be a side or back kick which is off target until the hooking motion begins. This kick is powerful since it employs the heel of the foot as the striking surface and is usually aimed to the side of the head or face. The hook kick is usually executed from a back stance or horseback stance.

HOOK KICK

(1) Assume a back stance as your opponent moves in with a punch. (2) Lean back on your rear leg (in this stance, the left leg) and raise your right leg and extend it out as if de-

livering a side or back kick, but with your target behind your heel. (3) Hook your heel backward by bending your knee sharply, striking the opponent's head.

WHEEL KICK

The wheel kick is useful in catching your opponent unaware since it appears to be a front kick (knee straight) which is off target until your kicking leg swings toward the target. This kick is very powerful but difficult to control and focus on the target because of the speed and momentum of the swinging motion.

The striking surface is the heel or the outer edge of the foot and is usually aimed to the side of the head or face. The wheel kick is usually executed from a back stance.

WHEEL KICK

(1) From a back stance, raise your kicking leg (in this case, the right) inward across your body and up in an arc. Your toes are bent upward and the knee is locked. (2) The heel and instep should be tensed, and as you

raise your kicking leg the target
should be to the side of your heel. (3)
Swing your leg outward, completing
the arc and striking through the
target, and continue your motion
until your foot is back on the ground.

CRESCENT KICKS

The crescent kick is effective in striking a short range target and can be used as a block, or as a sweeping technique. The striking surface is the arch of the foot. As a short range striking technique the crescent kick is usually aimed at the face when an opponent is in

INSIDE CRESCENT KICK

Raise the kicking leg up and out, knee bent and toes bent up. Hook your kicking leg inward, with your knees still bent, striking your opponent with the arch of your foot.

a low position. As a block it can be used against a middle punch or a front kick. It can also be used to sweep the opponent's leg and break his balance. The crescent kick is executed in the same manner for all three purposes.

OUTSIDE CRESCENT KICK

Raise the kicking leg up and inside, hooking your leg outward, using the outside edge of your foot as the striking surface, then follow through, bringing your leg out and back down.

TURNING KICKS

The turning kick is an advanced technique used to catch your opponent by surprise. Most kicks are executed either directly forward or to the side, but this kick is delivered while your body is turned backward. This kick is used to confuse your opponent and to strike your target at a greater distance. While turning, the head and upper body should spin in one smooth motion but the head should turn faster. Immediately after completing the turning motion, four types of kicks (side, back, hook and wheel) can be executed. The turning motion is used in the same manner before executing any one of the kicks mentioned. The turning hook kick is illustrated below as an example of how to execute a turning kick.

TURNING HOOK KICK

(1) Face your opponent in a back stance. (2) Spin to the right on your left foot, raising your right knee to waist level. (3) Your head must spin around slightly ahead of the rest of your body so that you can eye your opponent just before delivering the kick. At this point you should begin to

extend your kicking leg (4) to the left of your target (his right) and then execute a hook kick (5) by bending the leg at the knee sharply and kicking through the target, striking your opponent with your heel. Your body leans backward on your supporting foot.

JUMPING KICKS

The jumping kick is an advanced technique used for a surprise attack to strike a target high above you or at a great distance. It is an effective technique to use in fighting a taller opponent or in jumping over an obstacle to reach your target. If it is properly executed, the jumping kick is a very fast and powerful kick because you are mak-

JUMPING HIGH FRONT KICK

(1) From a ready position, (2) run toward your target until you are within striking distance, then plant your kicking foot (in this case, the left) and push your body (3&4) as high as possible off the ground. Your right leg should be high, knee bent sharply, then switch your legs in mid-air (5) at the highest point of your jump so that your kicking leg is forward. (6) Launch a front kick before your other leg touches the ground.

ing full use of your body's weight and momentum. There are several types of jumping kicks, commonly combined with the basic kicks like the front, side, round and hook kicks. This section illustrates three types.

ONE STEP JUMPING KICK

(1) From a ready position, (2) run toward your target until you are within striking distance. Push off with the foot opposite the one you intend to kick with (in this case, push off with your left foot) and (3) simultaneously raise your

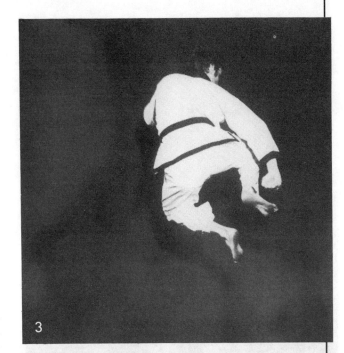

kicking leg high, knee bent sharply, preparing to execute the kick. (4) Thrust a side kick at your target before your other leg touches the ground. This one step technique may also be used with any of the other basic kicks.

JUMPING KICK
(Standing Position)

(1) From a ready position, jump up in the air (2) with both feet, keeping both knees as high as possible, sharply bent, in preparation to kick. Raise your kicking leg higher than the other one. (3) Launch a

round kick (or any of the other basic kicks) at your target before your other leg touches the ground. You may execute this technique with either the front foot or back foot.

SPARRING TECHNIQUES

There are five different stages to learning sparring techniques: three step sparring, two step sparring, one step sparring, prearranged sparring and free sparring. Three step sparring and one step sparring should be reviewed and studied from Volume I before learning the advanced techniques in this chapter.

One step sparring requires the application of basic blocking and attacking techniques. On the advanced level, a greater variety of combinations, advanced counterattacks and multiple kicking techniques should be practiced to provide a foundation before the student is ready for free sparring.

On the prearranged sparring level, the student arranges a format of attack and defense which he practices with a partner to simulate free sparring.

Free sparring is the final stage. The dynamic and unstructured combat situation requires the student to apply a great deal of knowledge and fighting skill automatically without preparation. Strength, speed, accuracy and especially control are needed to prevent possible injuries. Before a student attempts free sparring he must master all the basic and advanced levels of three step, two step, one step and prearranged sparring.

Relaxation while sparring is important for maintaining flexibility, reflexes and stamina. In advanced free sparring, light, controlled contact to the face and body are allowed. However, hand contact to the face should be exercised with caution and contact with the foot should be practiced with firm control.

DEFENSE AND COUNTERATTACKS

Before sparring, it is important that the student practice a variety of counterattacking techniques immediately after executing blocking techniques, because some counterattacks are specifically suited to follow certain blocks. It is recommended that the student learn several well coordinated combinations of block-and-counterattack. The student should practice these combinations so that they can be used in free sparring.

Basic defense and reverse punching techniques such as the low block reverse punch, high block reverse punch, and knife hand block reverse punch are covered in Volume I. The student should review and study these techniques from Volume I before learning the advanced combinations covered in this chapter. Two examples of defense and counterattack combinations follow.

EXAMPLE ONE

(1) Beginning from a ready stance, (2&3) step forward with the left leg into a forward stance and execute a

Continued on next page

3

high knife hand block with the left hand. Your right fist is palm up at your waist. Maintain the same hand position as you (4) execute a right front kick. (5&6) As you bring your right leg down into a right back stance, execute an outside middle block with the right hand. (7) Shift into a right forward stance and execute a left reverse punch to the face.

5

EXAMPLE TWO

(1) Beginning from a ready stance, (2&3) step forward with your left leg into a forward stance and execute a high X-block, right wrist over the left. Draw your palms toward your right side and (4&5) execute a right front kick. Your right fist is now palm up at the waist, and your left fist is palm in just above the right one. (6&7) As you

Continued on next page

7

bring your right leg down into a forward stance, draw your right hand back and execute a high knife hand strike, palm up. (8) Execute a left reverse punch to the chest.

8

THREE STEP SPARRING

On the advanced three step sparring level, the defender asks his attacker to execute specific attacking techniques so that the defender can practice the appropriate blocking techniques. Through this type of practice, the defender has the opportunity to practice various blocking techniques that he has learned previously. Blocking techniques can be either the execution in a series of a single blocking technique, (for example, three middle blocks or three knife hand middle blocks), or it can be a combination of two or three different blocking techniques.

In the next step, the attacker informs the defender of which attacking techniques he will execute. Then the defender should be able to apply the appropriate blocking techniques automatically. This type of practice provides the defender with an opportunity to improve his reflexes and coordination in applying blocking techniques.

In the final step of three step sparring, after the defender has executed his final block, he practices counterattacking techniques such as the various punching, striking and kicking techniques he has previously learned.

The student can vary the application of counterattacking techniques in the following manner.

1. A counterattack can be executed after each of the three blocks; for example, a left hand high block with a right hand high punch can be repeated three times.
2. Three different blocking and counterattacking combinations can be executed; for example, a left hand high block with a right hand high punch, a right knife hand middle block with a left spear hand thrust to the stomach, and a knife hand high X-block with a front kick.
3. Counterattacking techniques can be executed after applying only two blocks, then shifting position to avoid the third attack before delivering a counterattack.

The following is an example of three step sparring.

THREE STEP SPARRING

(1) Face your opponent in a ready position and (2) prepare for his attack as he assumes a forward stance. (3) As your opponent steps in with a right middle punch, step back into a right back stance and execute an outside middle block with your left hand. (4) Counter his left

middle punch by stepping back into a right forward stance and blocking with a right upward palm heel block. (5) As your opponent steps forward with another right middle punch, counterattack with a right side kick to his abdomen.

TWO STEP SPARRING

Two step sparring is the next step of learning after three step sparring. It is practiced in a similar manner as three step sparring. The defender asks his attacker to execute two specific attacking techniques, (for example, a right hand high punch and a left round kick). The defender then practices the application of one or more blocking and counterattacking techniques.

TWO STEP SPARRING

(1) Face your opponent in a ready stance. (2) As your opponent attacks with a right middle punch, step back into a right forward stance and execute a left palm heel block. (3) As your opponent delivers a

This type of training is an intermediate step which helps the student develop a better sense of combat and a sense of direction for quickly positioning himself in order to deliver the appropriate counterattacking techniques. The following is an example of two step sparring.

left roundhouse kick, step back into a horseback stance and execute a high block with your right hand. (4) Counterattack by pivoting on your right foot and delivering a left front kick to his abdomen.

ONE STEP SPARRING

There are two approaches to practicing advanced one step sparring. In one, the defender asks his partner to execute specific attacking techniques. In the other, the attacker informs the defender of which techniques he will attack with. In either case, the attacker advances only once with a technique which the defender must either block or avoid and immediately follow with an appropriate counterattack. (In most cases when no specific attack is mentioned by

ONE STEP SPARRING

(1) Face your partner in a ready position. (2) As he attacks with a right punch, step back into a left forward stance and execute a left high block. (3) Step behind your opponent's right leg into a horseback stance and deliver a knife hand strike to his neck. (4&5) Reach behind his right leg with your right hand and lift his leg quickly while pushing forward with your left hand, upsetting his balance and throwing him to the ground. (6) Deliver a low front kick with your right leg to his abdomen when he is down.

either partner, a high punch is commonly executed.) This type of training requires that the student be able to decide quickly upon the appropriate combination of block and counterattack, demanding speed and flexibility.

Basic one step sparring techniques are covered in Volume I and should be reviewed before using the blocks and counterattacks in this book. The following is an example of one step sparring.

PREARRANGED FREE SPARRING

The practice of prearranged free sparring is the final stage of preparation for free sparring. On this level the student simulates a combat situation by practicing a predetermined series of attack and defense techniques with a partner. Prearranged free sparring prepares the student for the free sparring level by increasing his coordination, accuracy, control and combinations of blocking, attacking, and counterattacking techniques.

The practice of prearranged free sparring can take two forms.

In one form, one student assumes the role of the attacker and advances toward the defender while executing a predetermined sequence of techniques. The defender retreats while applying a prearranged series of defensive techniques, in order to give his opponent an opportunity to execute his attacking techniques. When the sequence is completed, the students then reverse roles and repeat the exercise in the opposite direction.

In another form of prearranged free sparring, both partners participate on an equal basis. Each student attacks and defends spontaneously as in actual free sparring but the use of techniques is limited to those specifically prescribed by the instructor, for example, the use of punches only, or specific kicking techniques.

It is recommended that the student begin practicing this type of exercise by advancing against an imaginary opponent. This provides him with an opportunity to learn a combination of attacking techniques so that he can develop a well-rounded and smoothly executed attack.

When the student is ready to practice his techniques with a partner he must work on coordinating his movements with those of his partner. He should practice moving backward and forward at the same speed as his opponent. Then the speed should gradually be increased so that as the defender blocks each attack, the attacker will be forced to deliver a greater variety of techniques, in faster sequence, in order to get past the defensive blocks.

FREE SPARRING

Free sparring is the most dynamic sparring level since it simulates an actual combat situation. In this stage the choice and use of combinations of attacking and defensive techniques depends entirely upon the student's judgment and his ability to determine the appropriate fighting strategy required to meet his opponent. The student's choice of fighting techniques must vary with the size, distance and ability of his opponent.

It is recommended that the student first practice by himself to develop a variety of offensive and defensive stances and combinations of attacking and counterattacking techniques. During this practice the student should visualize an imaginary opponent so that he can improve the aim and focus of his techniques.

When the student has progressed sufficiently so that he can enter a combat situation with an actual opponent, he should begin by delivering basic attacking techniques in order to develop speed, coordination and accuracy. He should study his opponent's reactions to these attacks and then modify his basic techniques, (for example, by changing the angle of his movements in kicking or twisting his hip differently) after he has estimated the appropriate angle of attack, distance and height needed to be effective against this particular opponent.

The student must also be aware of the importance of executing an effective block with a counterattack. To deliver an effective counterattack the student must surprise his opponent. He must take advantage of his opponent's weak points and deliver his counterattack to an area which is unprotected while the opponent is concentrating on delivering either a single technique or a combination of techniques.

The following is an example of free sparring:

FREE SPARRING

(1) You and your opponent face off in a left back stance position, ready to move quickly into an attacking or defensive move. (2) As your opponent tries a front kick with

his right leg, deliver a low kick block with your right leg to his shin, then (3&4) pivot on your left foot and execute a high round-house kick to you opponent's head.

FORMS

The forms were designed to provide a means of practicing defensive and offensive techniques in a series of continuous movements. They were intended to train students to defend themselves against more than one opponent and to fight in any direction for as long as necessary without tiring. Thus, the forms are essential elements of the art of tae kwon do. It is important to practice them with patience and concentration to increase your accuracy, coordination, speed, power, endurance and balance.

The Kicho forms and the first three Palgwe forms are covered in Volume I. This chapter covers three additional Palgwe forms. The Palgwe forms symbolize that the universe is infinite and unknowable and that there is some integrating force of cosmic cohesion which keeps it in order. The forms signify the constancy of truth and the truth of constant change. The principle of Palgwe is that one who knows himself and his environment will find the path of harmony between the changeable forces of the world in which he lives.

This chapter also covers the five Ki-bon forms which are the combat forms, Chul-Ki Cho Dan, and Bal-Seck forms, which are required for the first dan promotion.

Note: The Korean Tae Kwon Do Association offically changed the spelling from *Palgye* to *Palgwe.*

PALGWE SA-CHANG
(No.4)

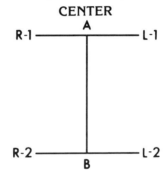

CENTER

R-1 ——————— A ——————— L-1

R-2 ——————— L-2
B

PALGWE SA-CHANG #4

(Ready) Assume a ready stance at center A. (1A) Turn your face 90 degrees to L1, preparing to step with your left foot toward L1, both fists drawn to your right hip ready to

Ready
Stance

1A

Continued on next page

145

1B

block. (1B) Step toward L1 into a left back stance simultaneously executing a double hand high and middle block (refer to Chapter 5 on blocking techniques). (2) Maintain the back stance while twisting your body toward L1, at the same time pull your left fist in toward your right shoulder and bring your right hand down to execute an uppercut strike to the chin. (3A&3B) Draw your left foot from the back stance into a ready stance and simultaneously execute a left knife hand strike, palm down, at shoulder level. (4A&4B) Bring your

3A

2

3B

4A

Continued on next page

4B

left foot back to center A next to your right foot, simultaneously turning your face 180 degrees toward R1, drawing both fists back to your left hip preparing to block. Step out toward R1 with your right foot into a right back stance, simultaneously executing a double hand high and middle block. (5) Maintain the back stance while twisting your body toward R1, at the same time pull your right fist in toward your left shoulder and bring your left hand down to execute an uppercut strike to the chin. (6A&6B) Draw your right foot from the back stance to the ready stance and simultaneously execute a right knife hand strike, palm down, at shoulder level. (7A) Bring your right foot back to center A at right angles to your left foot, simultaneously turning your face 90 degrees to the left toward B,

6A

5

6B

7A

Continued on next page

7B

palms open ready to block. (7B) Step forward toward B with your left foot into a left back stance, simultaneously executing a middle knife hand block with your left hand. (8A) Execute a right front kick and then (8B) step forward toward B with your right foot into a right front stance, executing a left palm heel block downward and a right spear hand thrust to the midsection simultaneously (your left hand is under your right elbow). (9A) Begin pivoting on the ball of your right foot to your left, drawing the left foot around your right foot in an arc. At the same time, pull your right palm behind your back at waist level (left palm in the crook of your right elbow) and maintain eye contact toward B. (9B) Continue your 360-degree turn to the left until you are facing B again, stepping out toward B into a left front

8B

8A

9A

9B

Continued on next page

9C

stance (9C) and simultaneously executing a left side hammer strike at
shoulder level. (10) Step forward
toward B with your right foot into a
right front stance, simultaneously
executing a right middle punch (yell).
(11A&11B) Pivot on the ball of your
right foot 270 degrees to your left
until you are facing R2, stepping out
with your left foot into a left back
stance and executing a double hand
high and middle block. (12) Maintain
the back stance while twisting your
body toward R2, at the same time
pulling your left fist in toward your
right shoulder and your right hand
down to execute an uppercut strike

11A

10

11B

12

Continued on next page

13

to the chin. (13) Draw your left foot from the back stance into a ready stance, simultaneously executing a left knife hand strike, palm down, at shoulder level. (14A&14B) Bring your left foot back to center B next to your right foot, simultaneously turning your face 180 degrees toward L2, drawing both hands back to your left hip preparing to block. Step out toward L2 with your right foot into a right back stance, simultaneously executing a double hand high and middle block. (15) Maintain the back stance while twisting your body toward L2, at the same time pull your right fist in toward your left shoulder and bring your left fist down to excecute an uppercut strike to the chin. (16) Draw your right foot from the back stance to a ready stance and simultaneously execute a right knife hand strike, palm down, at

14B

14A

15

16

Continued on next page

17A

shoulder level. (17A) Bring your right foot back to center B at right angles to your left foot, simultaneously turning your face 90 degrees to the left toward A, palms open ready to block. (17B) Step forward toward A with your left foot into a left back stance, simultaneously executing a middle knife hand block with your left hand. (18A) Execute a right front kick and then (18B) step forward toward A with your right foot into a right front stance, executing a left palm heel block downward and a right spear hand thrust to the midsection (your left hand is under your right elbow). (19A) Begin pivoting on the ball of your right foot to your left, drawing your left foot around behind your right foot in an arc. At the same time, pull your right palm up to ear level and maintain eye contact toward A.

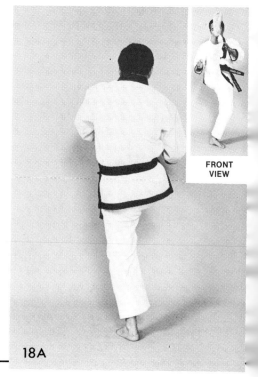

FRONT
VIEW

18A

17B

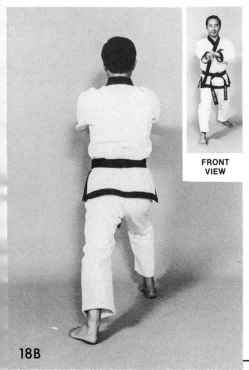

18B

FRONT
VIEW

19A

Continued on next page

19B

(19B) Continue your 360-degree turn to the left until you are (19C) facing A again, stepping out toward A with your left foot into a left front stance, simultaneously executing a left side hammer strike at shoulder level. (20) Step forward toward A with your right foot into a right front stance, simultaneously executing a right middle punch (yell). (21A&21B) Pivot on the ball of your right foot 270 degrees, stepping out toward L1 with your left foot into a horseback stance, simultaneously executing a left low block.

20

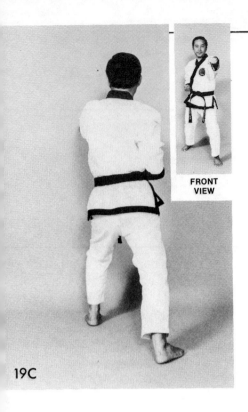

FRONT VIEW

19C

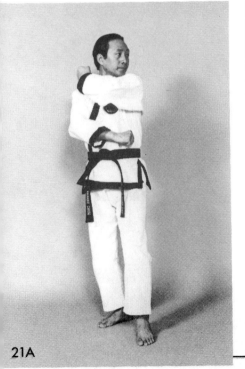

21A

21B

Continued on next page

22

(22) Step toward L1 with your left foot into a left front stance and execute a reverse punch with your right fist. (23A&23B) Draw your left foot back toward center A into a ready stance and turn your face 180 degrees facing R1. Draw your right fist back to your left shoulder and step forward toward R1 with your right foot into a horseback stance, simultaneously executing a right low block. (24) Step toward R1 with your right foot into a right front stance, and execute a reverse punch with your left fist. (Stop) Draw your right foot back to center A as you pivot 90 degrees on your left foot, facing B in the ready stance.

23B

23A

24

Stop

PALGWE O-CHANG
(No. 5)

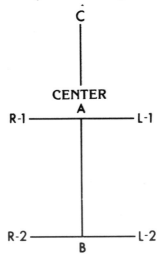

C

CENTER
A

R-1 ———————— L-1

R-2 ———————— L-2
B

Ready Stance

PALGWE O-CHANG #5

(Ready) Assume ready stance at center A. (1) Step back toward C with your left foot into a right front stance, simultaneously executing a scissor block (left fist executing a middle

1

Continued on next page

2

block, your right fist a low block). (2) Step toward L1 with your left foot into a left back stance, executing a low knife hand block with your left hand. (3) Step toward L1 with your right foot into a right back stance, simultaneously executing a middle knife hand block with your right hand. (4) Step backward with your right foot into a left back stance (still facing L1) simultaneously executing a downward palm heel block at chest level with your left hand. (5) Step forward toward L1 with your right foot into a right front stance, simultaneously executing a right hand middle punch. (6) Pivot 180 degrees to the right on your left heel, stepping toward R1 with your right foot into a right back stance, simultaneously executing a low knife hand block with your right

4

3

5

6

Continued on next page

7

hand. (7) Step toward R1 with your left foot into a left back stance, simultaneously executing a middle knife hand block with your left hand. (8) Step backward with your left foot into a right back stance (still facing R1), simultaneously executing a downward palm heel block at chest level with your right hand. (9) Step toward R1 with your left foot into a left front stance, simultaneously executing a left hand middle punch. (10) Pivot 90 degrees to your left stepping toward B with your left foot into a left front stance and simultaneously executing a scissor block (left hand executes a low block, your right hand a middle block). (11) Step toward B with your right foot into a right front stance, simultaneously executing a right double hand middle

9

8

10

11

Continued on next page

12

block. (12) Step toward B with your left foot into a left front stance, simultaneously executing a left double hand middle block. (13) Step toward B with your right foot into a right front stance and execute a left palm heel block downward and a right spear hand thrust to the midsection (yell). (14) Pivot 270 degrees to your left on the ball of your right foot, stepping toward R2 with your left foot into a left front stance, simultaneously executing a left hand middle block (inside to outside). (15A&15B) Maintaining the left front stance, execute in rapid succession a right hand reverse punch and a

14

13

15A

15B

Continued on next page

left hand middle punch. (16) Pivot 90 degrees to the right on the ball of your right foot (so your body faces A), lifting your left foot to your right knee in a crane stance. Simultaneously, bring both fists to your right hip (right fist palm up at the waist, left fist palm in over your right fist). Your face is still turned toward R2. (17A) Execute a left side kick toward R2 and a left hand side punch parallel to your kicking leg. (17B) Step toward R2 with your left foot into a left front stance, simultaneously twisting your hip and shoulders toward R2 and executing a right elbow target strike against your left palm. (18) Step toward R2 with your right foot into a right back stance, simultaneously executing a middle knife hand block with your right hand. (19) Pivot 180 degrees to your right on your left heel, stepping toward L2 with your right foot into a right front stance, simultaneously executing a right hand middle block (inside to outside). (20A&20B) Main-

16

18

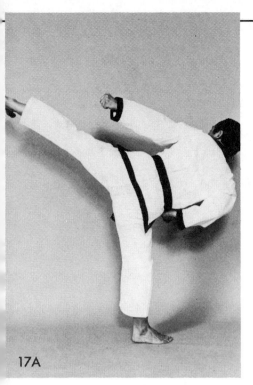

17A

17B

19

20A

Continued on next page

taining the right front stance, execute in rapid succession a left hand reverse punch and a right hand middle punch. (21) Pivot 90 degrees to the left on the ball of your left foot (so that your body faces A), lifting your right foot to your left knee in a crane stance. Simultaneously, bring both fists near your left hip (your left fist palm up at the waist, your right fist palm in over your left). Your face is still turned toward L2. (22A) Execute a right side kick toward L2 and a right side punch parallel to your kicking leg. (22B) Step toward L2 with your right foot into a right front stance, simultaneously twisting your hip and shoulders toward L2 and executing a left elbow target strike against your right palm. (23) Step toward L2 with your left foot into a left back stance, simultaneously executing a middle knife hand block with your left hand. (24) Pivot 90 degrees to the left on the ball of your right foot and step toward A with your left foot into a left front stance, simultaneously executing a scissor block (the low block with your left fist, the middle block with your

20B

22B

21

22A

23

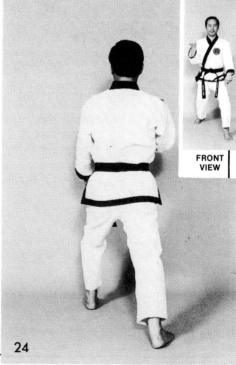

FRONT
VIEW

24

Continued on next page

173

25

right). (25) Step toward A with your right foot into a right back stance, simultaneously executing a right double hand low block, palm down (left hand assisting, palm up). (26) Step toward A with your left foot into a left back stance, simultaneously executing a left double hand low block, palm down (right hand assisting, palm up). (27) Step toward A with your right foot into a right front stance, simultaneously executing a right middle punch (yell). (28) Pivot 270 degrees to the left on the ball of your right foot, stepping toward L1 with your left foot into a left back stance, simultaneously executing a low knife hand block with your left hand. (29) Step toward L1 with your right foot into a right back stance, simultaneously executing a middle knife hand block with your right hand. (30) Step backward with your right foot into a left back stance (still facing L1) and execute a downward palm heel block at chest level

28

26

27

29

30

Continued on next page

31

with your left hand. (31) Step toward L1 with your right foot into a right front stance, simultaneously executing a right hand middle punch. (32) Pivot 180 degrees to the right on your left heel, stepping toward R1 with your right foot into a right back stance and executing a low knife hand block with your right hand. (33) Step toward R1 with your left foot into a left back stance, simultaneously executing a middle knife hand block with your left hand. (34) Step backward with your left foot into a right back stance (still facing R1) and execute a downward palm heel block at chest level with your right hand. (35) Step toward R1 with your left foot into a left front stance and execute a left hand middle punch. (Stop) Pivot 90 degrees to your left on your right foot, drawing your left foot to center A into a ready stance facing B.

34

32

33

35

Stop

PALGWE YOOK-CHANG
(No. 6)

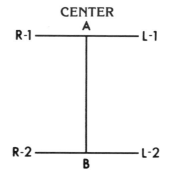

Ready
Stance

PALGWE YOOK-CHANG #6

(Ready) Assume ready stance at center A. (1) Step toward L1 with your left foot into a left back stance, simultaneously executing a left knife hand

1

Continued on next page

2A

block. (2A&2B) Execute a right front kick then step toward L1 with your right foot into a right front stance, simultaneously executing a right hand middle punch. (3) Pivot 180 degrees to the right on your left heel and step toward R1 with your right foot into a right back stance, simultaneously executing a right knife hand block. (4A&4B) Execute a left front kick, then step toward R1 with your left foot into a left front stance,

3

2B

4A

4B

Continued on next page

5

simultaneously executing a left hand middle punch. (5) Pivot 90 degrees to the left on your right foot, stepping toward B with your left foot into a left front stance, simultaneously executing a low left hand block. (6) Maintain the left front stance and execute a rising knife hand block with your left hand at the same time you deliver a knife hand strike (palm up) to the neck with your right hand (outside to inside). (7A) Maintain this hand position while executing a right front kick toward B. (7B&7C) Leap toward B with your right foot, drawing your left foot behind the right into a right cross stance. At the same time, execute a right double hand back fist strike to the face, left hand assisting

7A

6

7B

7C

Continued on next page

8

(yell). (8) Pivot 270 degrees to the left on the balls of your feet, stepping toward R2 with the left foot into a left back stance and simultaneously executing a low knife hand block with the left hand. (9) Step toward R2 with your left foot into a left front stance, simultaneously executing a middle spread block (blocking with the outer edge of the forearm, palms out). (10A-10C) Execute a right front kick toward R2, step forward with your right foot into a right front stance and execute in rapid succession a right hand middle punch followed by a left

10A

9

10B

10C

Continued on next page

11

reverse punch. (11) Pivot 180 degrees
to the right on your left heel, stepping
toward L2 with your right foot into a
right back stance, simultaneously
executing a low knife hand block with
your right hand. (12) Step toward L2
with your right foot into a right front
stance, simultaneously executing a
middle spread block. (13A-13C) Execute a left front kick toward L2, step
forward with your left foot into a left
front stance and execute in rapid
succession a left hand middle punch

13A

12

13B

13C

Continued on next page

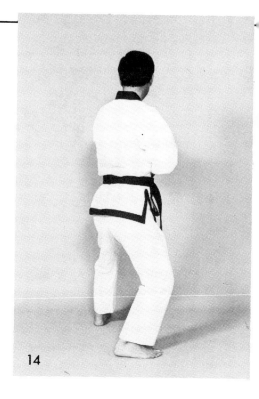

14

followed by a right reverse punch. (14) Pivot 90 degrees to the left on your right foot, stepping toward A with your left foot into a left back stance, simultaneously executing a middle knife hand block with your left hand. (15) Step toward A with your left foot into a left front stance and execute a rising knife hand block with your left hand at the same time thrusting a right palm heel strike forward at chin level. (16A&16B) Maintaining this hand position, execute a right front kick, then step toward A with your right foot into a right front stance, simultaneously executing a right back fist strike to the face (yell). (17A&17B) Maintain this hand position and execute a left front kick,

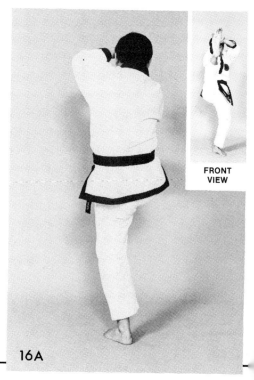

FRONT VIEW

16A

15

16B

FRONT
VIEW

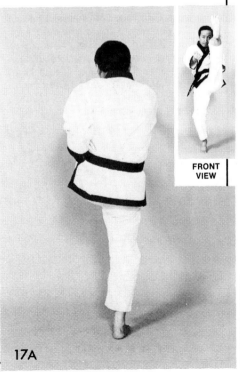

17A

FRONT
VIEW

Continued on next page

17B

then step toward A with your left foot
into a left front stance, simultaneously executing a high left hand block.
(18A&18B) Execute a right side kick
and a right hand side punch simultaneously toward C (your punch is
parallel to your kicking leg). (18C)
Step toward C with your right foot
into a right back stance, simultaneously executing a middle knife hand
block with your right hand. (19) Pivot
180 degrees to the left toward A on
your left heel assuming a left back
stance, simultaneously executing a
left knife hand block. (Stop) Draw
your right foot forward toward center
A next to your left foot and assume a
ready stance facing B.

FRONT
VIEW

18C

18A

18B

19

Stop

KI-BON (No. 1)

```
        C
        |
CENTER
        A
        |
        |
        |
        B
```

Ready Stance

(Ready Stance) Assume a ready position at center A facing B. (1) Slide your right foot backward toward C into a left front stance, simultaneously executing a low block with your left hand. (2) Step toward B with your right foot into a right front stance, simultaneously executing a middle punch with your right hand. (3) Step toward B with your left foot into a left front stance, simultaneously executing a high block with your left hand. (4) Step again toward B with your right foot into a right front stance and simultaneously execute a right hand middle punch (yell). (5) Pivot to your left 180 degrees toward C on the ball of your right foot and step with your left foot into a left back stance, simultaneously executing a low knife hand block with the left hand. (6) Step toward C with your right foot into a right back stance, simultaneously executing a middle knife hand block with your right hand. (7) Step toward C with your left foot into a left back stance, simultaneously executing a high knife hand block with your left hand. (8) Grab the arm of your opponent with your left hand while stepping toward C with your right foot into a right front stance, simultaneously executing a middle punch with the right hand (yell). (Stop) Pivot to your left 180 degrees toward B on the ball of your right foot, sliding your left foot backward to center A into the ready stance.

3

7

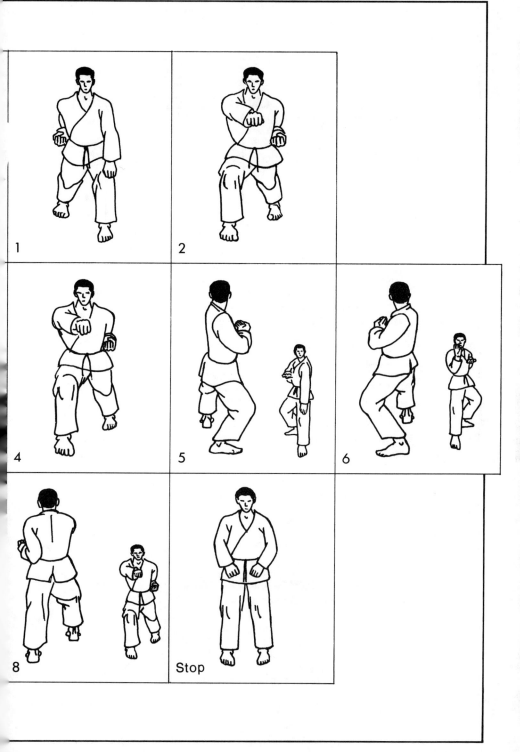

1

2

4

5

6

8

Stop

KI-BON
(No. 2)

```
        C
        |
CENTER
        A
        |
        |
        |
        |
        B
```

Ready Stance

3

6

(Ready Stance) Assume a ready position at center A facing B. (1) Slide your right foot backward toward C into a left back stance, simultaneously executing an outside middle block with the left hand. (2) Raise your right foot toward B with your knee bent at waist level, simultaneously raising both hands to your upper right. Your right fist is at face level, palm out, and your left fist is in front of your right shoulder, palm in. (3) Pivot 90 degrees to the left on the ball of your left foot while stepping down toward B with your right foot into a horseback stance, simultaneously executing a double hand block (your left hand executes a downward middle block, your right hand an inside middle block). Apply a strong twisting motion of the right hip with this step. (4) Pivot 90 degrees to the right toward B on the ball of your right foot, raising your left foot forward with the knee bent at waist level. Raise both hands to your upper left, your left fist at face level, palm out, and your right fist in front of your left shoulder, palm in. (5) Pivot 90 degrees to the right on the ball of your right foot while stepping down toward B with your left foot into a horseback stance, simultaneously executing a double hand block (your left hand executes an inside middle block, your right hand a downward middle block). (6) Keeping your left foot in place, slide your right foot toward C into a right back stance, simultaneously executing a low knife hand block with the right hand. Your left hand is also in the knife hand position, held palm up at the ribs. (7A&7B) Slide your left foot toward C into a left front stance, simultaneously executing a low cross block with your left fist over your right fist, palms

Continued on next page

out. (8A) Slide your right foot forward and place it next to your left foot as you pivot 90 degrees on the ball of your left foot, bringing both hands up simultaneously, your right hand open and under your left shoulder, palm down, and your left fist over your right shoulder, palm down. Your face should still be turned toward C. (8B) Keeping your left foot in place, slide your right foot toward C into a horseback stance, simultaneously executing a high ridge hand block with the right hand, palm up. (9) Keeping both feet in place, execute a left elbow target strike toward C at chest level, striking your open right hand with your left elbow (the left fist is palm down). (10) Step toward C with your left foot into a left front stance, pivoting on the ball of your right foot and simultaneously executing a middle punch with the left hand. (11) Pivot 180 degrees to the left toward B on the ball of your right foot, stepping with your left foot into a left front stance and simultaneously executing a side hammer strike at shoulder level with your left hand, palm down. (12A&12B) Keeping both feet in place, execute a reverse punch with your right hand and follow immediately with a left middle punch. (13) Keeping both feet in place, execute a high open hand block with your left hand while simultaneously delivering a right hand middle punch (yell). (Stop) Keep your right foot in place, slide your left foot backward to center A and end facing B in the ready stance.

8B

9

11

12A

13

Stop

KI-BON (No. 3)

C
|
CENTER
A
|
|
B

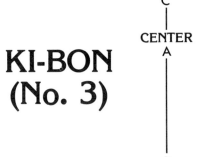

(Ready Stance) Assume a ready stance at center A facing B. (1) Slide your right foot backward toward C into a left front stance, simultaneously executing a low block with the left hand. (2) Keeping both feet in place, execute a left hand high block. (3) Keeping both feet in place, execute a right hand outside middle block. (4) Keeping both feet in place, execute a left hand middle punch. (5) Keeping both feet in place, execute a right hand reverse punch. (6) Step toward B with your right foot into a right front stance, simultaneously executing a right hand low block. (7) Keeping both feet in place, execute a right hand high block. (8) Keeping both feet in place, exe-

Ready
Stance

3

6

1

2

4

5

7

8

Continued on next page

cute a left hand outside middle block. (9) Keeping both feet in place, execute a right hand middle punch. (10) Keeping both feet in place, execute a left hand reverse punch. (11) Keeping both hands in the previous position, execute a left front kick and, without bringing your foot down again, (12A) pivot 90 degrees to the right on the ball of your right foot, bringing your left foot to the side of your right knee. Simultaneously, bring both fists to your right side near your waist, with your right fist palm up and your left fist palm in over your right fist. Your face remains facing B. (12B) Immediately, execute a side kick with the left leg and a side punch with the left fist toward B. (13A) Bring your left foot down next to your right foot and pivot 90 degrees to the right on the ball of your left foot, facing A. Bring your right foot up to the side of your left knee and simultaneously bring both fists back to your right side near your waist, right fist palm up and left fist palm in above the right fist. (13B) Execute a right back kick and right punch toward B. (14) Step down toward B with your right foot into a horseback stance (body faces L and head faces B). Simultaneously execute a right hand low block. (15) Keeping both feet in place, execute a right knife hand strike at shoulder level, palm down. (16A) Keeping both feet in place, turn your body to the right facing B and at the same time, bring your right fist to your waist, palm up.

9

12A

14

Continued on next page

16B

(16B) Execute a right side punch toward B (body faces L again) and yell. (17) Pivoting 270 degrees to the right on the ball of your right foot, slide your left foot forward in an arc toward B into a right back stance (body faces R and head is turned 180 degrees to the right facing A). Simultaneously execute a right knife hand middle block. (18) Execute a left front kick. (19) Step down with your left foot toward A into a left front stance. Simultaneously execute a scissor block (left hand middle, right hand low). (20) Keeping both feet in place, execute an X-block (left fist over right fist, palms out). (21) Execute a right front kick. (22) Step down with your right foot into a right front stance. Simultaneously execute a scissor block (right hand middle, left hand low). (23) Keeping both feet in place, execute an X-block (right fist over left, palms out). (24) Slide your left foot forward into a left front stance, simultaneously executing a left hand middle punch (yell). (Stop) Pivot 180 degrees to the right toward B on the ball of your left foot. Slide your right foot back into a ready stance facing B at point A.

19

23

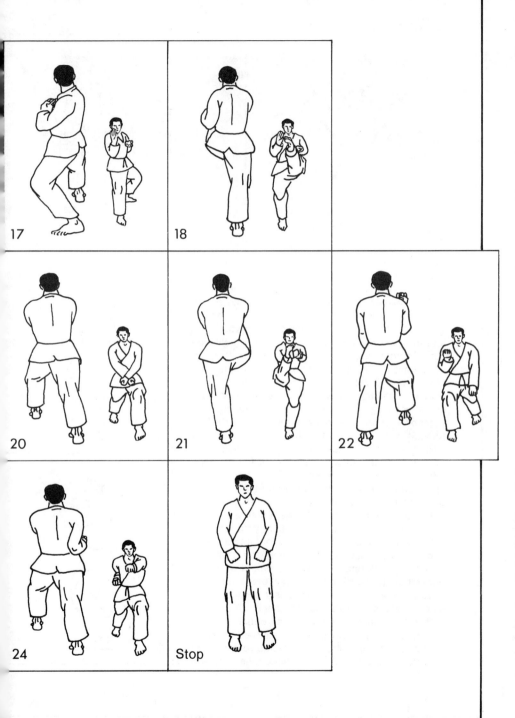

17

18

20

21

22

24

Stop

KI-BON
(No. 4)

```
        C
        |
 CENTER
        A
        |
        |
        |
        |
        B
```

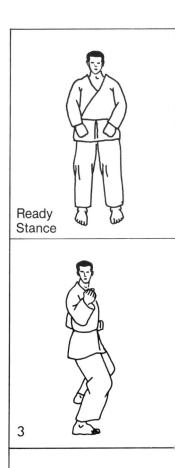

Ready Stance

(Ready Stance) Assume a ready position at center A facing B. (1) Slide your right foot backward toward C into a left front stance, simultaneously executing a left hand outside middle block. (2) Raise your right foot toward B, knee bent at waist level and body facing to the right. Simultaneously, raise both fists to face level, elbows bent 90 degrees and palms out. (3) Pivoting 90 degrees to the left on the ball of your left foot, step down toward B with your right foot into a horseback stance, simultaneously executing a right hand inside middle block. (4) Pivoting 90 degrees to the right on the ball of your right foot, step toward B with your left foot into a left front stance, simultaneously executing a downward cross block, right fist over left and palms out. (5A) Keeping your left foot in place, slide your right foot forward next to your left with the right foot at a 90-degree angle. Simultaneously, bring both fists to your right side at waist level, right fist palm up, left fist palm down. (5B) Keeping your right foot in place, step toward B with your left foot into a horseback stance, simultaneously executing a side punch at shoulder level with the left fist. (6) Pivot 180 degrees to the left on the ball of your left foot, stepping toward B with your right foot into a horseback stance. Simultaneously, execute a right elbow target strike, hitting your open left hand with your right elbow. (7) Keeping both feet in place, turn your head to face C and simultaneously execute a low block to the side with your left hand. (8) Keeping both feet in place, execute a hook punch with the right hand. (9) Pivot 90 degrees to your left toward C on the ball of your right foot and slide your left foot forward into a left front stance, simultaneously exe-

3

6

Continued on next page

cuting a high block with the left hand. (10) Keeping both feet in place, execute a high right hand reverse punch. (11) Step toward C with your right foot into a right front stance, simultaneously executing a high cross block, right hand over your left with the palms out. (12) Twist your wrists to the right and grab, pulling both fists to your right side while executing a left front kick. (13A&13B) Step down toward C with your left foot into a left front stance, simultaneously executing two high punches to the neck with your left hand. (14) Pivot 90 degrees to the left on the ball of your left foot and step toward C with your right foot into a horseback stance, simultaneously executing a side punch with the right fist. (15) Pivot 90 degrees to the left on the ball of your right foot, slide your left foot backward into a left cat stance and execute a right hammer fist strike (outside to inside) toward B. (16) Keeping your hands in position, execute a left front kick. (17) Step down with your left foot into a left back stance, simultaneously executing an open hand high block with the left hand, palm down. (18) Keeping both feet in place, execute a right hand reverse punch (yell). (Stop) Slide your left foot backward next to your right into a ready stance at center A facing B.

10

13A

16

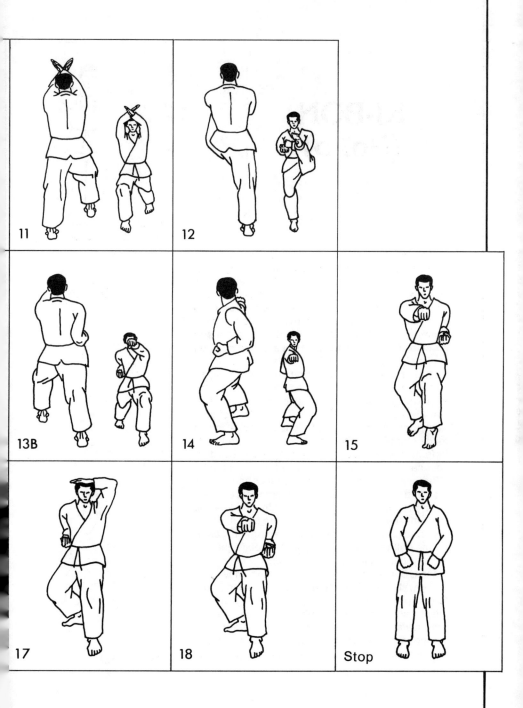

KI-BON (No. 5)

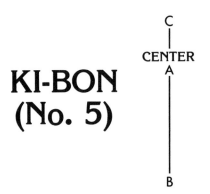

C
|
CENTER
A
|
|
|
|
B

Ready Stance

2A

3C

(Ready Position) Assume an informal stance (feet together) at position A facing B with your right fist directly in front of you at shoulder level, palm in and covered by the left hand. Your elbows are bent slightly forming an arc. (1A) Step slightly toward B with your left foot bringing both hands up and back toward your left with the right fist palm down and covered by your left hand. (1B) Leap toward B on your right foot into a right cross stance (your left foot is crossed directly behind your right foot) simultaneously executing a back fist strike to the face with your right fist, left hand open on your fist. (2A) Pivot to the left 90 degrees on the ball of your right foot, sliding your left foot toward A into a ready stance, simultaneously keeping both hands in front of your face, opening the right fist so that your hands are now palms out, left hand over right. (2B) Keeping both feet in place, raise both hands high in front of your head and thrust them outward in an arc, palms out, exhaling loudly and keeping the arms tensed until your elbows are bent at shoulder level. (3A) Pivot 90 degrees to the right toward B on the ball of your left foot, sliding your right foot slightly back and then forward into a right front stance. Simultaneously execute a high knife hand block with your right hand. (3B&3C) Keeping both feet in place, execute first a left and then a right spear hand thrust to the ribs, palms up. (4A&4B) Step toward B with your left foot into a left front stance, simultaneously executing first a left and then a right spear hand thrust to the ribs, palms up.

1A

1B

2B

3A

3B

4A

4B

(5) Keeping your left foot in place, execute a target crescent kick with the right foot, outside to inside, striking your open left hand with the inside arch of your right foot. (6) Keeping your left foot in place, step down toward the right with your right foot into a horseback stance facing B, simultaneously executing a right elbow target strike. (7) Keeping both feet in place, execute an outside middle block with the right hand, placing your left hand palm down on the inside of your right elbow. (8) Keeping both feet in place, execute a low block with your right hand, with your left hand now palm in on top of your right elbow. (9) Pivot 180 degrees to your left toward A on the ball of your right foot, sliding the left foot back and then forward in an arc into a left back stance. Simultaneously execute a low block with your left hand. (10) Step toward A with your right foot into a right back stance, simultaneously executing a low block with your right hand. (11) Step toward A with your left foot into a left back stance, simultaneously executing another low block with your left hand. (12) Keeping your left foot in place, slide your right foot forward and to the right toward L2 into a horseback stance facing A. Simultaneously, bring your right fist back to the waist, palm up. (13A&13B) Keeping your left foot in place, pivot 45 degrees on the ball of your right foot (your body also faces 45 degrees to the left) and simultaneously execute a high punch with your right fist. Follow immediately

5

8

12

Continued on next page

with a high block with the right hand. (14A&14B) Pivot 45 degrees to the right on the balls of both feet (your body turning a total of 90 degrees, now angled 45 degrees to your right) and execute rapidly a high left punch and then a high left block. (15) Pivot 45 degrees to the left on the balls of both feet (body turning a total of 90 degrees to the left) simultaneously executing a knife hand strike to the temple with the right hand, palm up. (16A) Keeping your left foot in place and your hands in the same position, execute a right front kick. (16B) Leap forward a step toward A on your right foot into a right cross stance (your left foot crossed directly behind your right foot), simultaneously executing a back fist strike to the face with your right hand (yell). (17) Pivot 270 degrees to the left on the ball of your right foot, sliding your left foot toward L1 into a left back stance and executing a middle knife hand block with your left hand. (18) Pivot 180 degrees to the right on the ball of your left foot, sliding your right foot slightly backward and to the right toward R1 into a right back stance. Simultaneously execute a middle knife hand block with your right hand. (19) Keeping your right foot in place, slide your left foot toward B into a left back stance (a longer step than usual, lowering your body more and your back knee also) simultaneously execute a left spear hand thrust to the head. (19B) Keeping both feet in place, execute a high knife hand block with your left hand. (Stop) Slide your left foot back next to your right foot into the informal stance at position A facing B. Your hands are returned to their starting position.

14A

16A

19A

14B

15

16B

17

18

19B

Stop

CHUL-KI CHO DAN (No. 1)

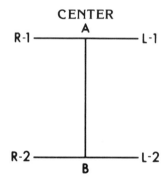

CHUL-KI CHO DAN

(Ready) Assume an informal stance facing B at center A, eyes focused straight ahead with both hands positioned in front of your waist, palms in, left hand placed over your right. (1) Rapidly raise your left foot in front of your right knee, simultaneously bending your right knee slightly and turning your face toward R. The hands are now in front of the left

Ready Stance

1

Continued on next page

2

knee, elbows slightly bent. (2) Keeping your right foot in place, step toward R with your left foot into a left cross stance, simultaneously raising both hands up; left fist is palm down in front of your right shoulder, your right palm open and underneath your left arm. (3) Keeping your left foot in place, step toward B with your right foot into a horseback stance, simultaneously executing a side ridge hand block with your right hand, palm up and elbow bent slightly at shoulder level (the blocking surface is the inner wrist of your forearm). (4) Execute a left elbow target strike, hitting your open right palm. (5) Remaining in place, with face turned toward B, execute a right elbow strike to the rear with your left fist placed palm in over your right fist. (6A&6B)

4

3

5

6A

Continued on next page

6B

Keeping both feet in place, turn your face toward L and execute a low side block with your left fist. (7) Execute a right hook punch to the midsection. (8) Keeping your left foot in place and hands in position, move your right foot toward L into a right cross stance. (9) Keeping your right foot in place (with your right knee locked straight), raise your left knee to waist level and turn your upper body toward L, simultaneously raising your left fist over your right arm at shoulder level, palm down in front of your right shoulder. (10) Step down toward L with your left foot into a horseback stance facing B, simultaneously executing a right back fist strike to the face. Maintaining the same position,

8

7

9

10

Continued on next page

11

(11) execute a scissor block (left fist delivers an outside middle block, your right fist a low block). (12) Keeping both feet in place, execute a left back fist strike to the rear, face level, twisting your upper body toward the target. (13) Again facing B, execute a left uppercut punch to the chin, right fist placed under your left elbow, palm down. (14A-14C) Keeping both

13

12

14A

14B

Continued on next page

14C

feet in place, turn your face 45 degrees to the left and execute an inside crescent kick at knee level with your left foot. Follow immediately by stepping toward L with your left foot in to a horseback stance and twisting your upper body 45 degrees to the left to deliver an outside middle block with your left fist (right fist under your left elbow, palm down). (15A-15C) Keeping both feet in place, turn your face 90 degrees to the right and execute an inside crescent kick at knee level with your right foot. Follow immediately by stepping toward R with your right foot into a horseback stance and twisting your upper body 90 degrees to deliver an inside middle block with your left fist (your right fist underneath your left elbow, palm down). (16) Keeping both feet in place, face B again and execute a right elbow strike to the rear, with your left fist palm in above your right

15B

15A

15C

16

Continued on next page

17

fist. (17) Execute a left side punch toward L, simultaneously executing a down block at chest level with your right fist (the blocking surface is the inside of your forearm). (18) Maintaining the horseback stance, raise your right fist until it is in front of your left shoulder (forearm is parallel to your shoulders) and bring your left hand across your chest underneath your right arm, palm down. (19) Execute a side ridge hand block toward L, palm up, with your elbow slightly bent. The blocking surface is the inner wrist of your forearm. (20) Maintaining the horseback stance, twist your body toward L and execute a right elbow target strike, hitting your open left palm with your right elbow. (21) Keeping both feet in place, face B again and execute a left elbow strike to the rear, with your right fist palm in above your left

19

18

20

21

Continued on next page

22A

wrist. (22A&22B) Keeping both feet in place, turn your face to the right toward R and execute a low side block with your right fist. (23) Execute a left hook punch to the midsection. (24) Keeping your right foot in place, step toward R with your left foot into a left cross stance. (25) Keeping your left foot in place (left knee locked straight), raise your right knee up to waist level, simultaneously turning your upper body toward R while still facing B. At the same time, raise your right arm over your left arm at shoulder level so that your right fist is palm down in front of your left shoulder. (26) Step down toward R with your right foot into a horseback stance facing B, simultaneously executing a

24

22B

23

25

26

Continued on next page

27

left back fist strike to the face. (27) Maintaining the horseback stance, execute a scissor block (right fist delivers an outside middle block, your left fist a low block). (28) Keeping both feet in place, execute a right back fist strike to the rear at face level, your upper body twisting to the right toward the target. (29) Keeping both feet in place, face B again and execute a right uppercut punch to the chin, with your left fist placed under your right elbow, palm down. (30A-30C) Turn your face 45 degrees to the right and execute an inside crescent kick at knee level with your right foot. Follow immediately by stepping toward R with your right foot into a horseback stance and twisting your upper body to the right to deliver an outside middle block with the right fist (left fist under the right elbow,

30A

28

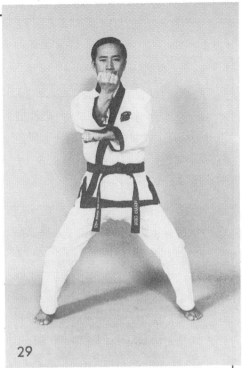

29

30B

30C

Continued on next page

palm down). (31A-31C) Keeping both feet in place, turn your face 90 degrees to the left and execute an inside crescent kick at knee level with your left foot. Follow immediately by stepping toward L with your left foot into a horseback stance and twisting your upper body to the left to deliver an inside middle block with your right fist (left fist under your right elbow, palm down). (32) Keeping both feet in place, turn toward B again and execute a left elbow strike to the rear, with your right fist palm in above your left fist. (33) Keeping both feet in place, execute a side punch toward R with your right fist, simultaneously executing a down block at chest level with your left fist (the blocking surface is the inside of your forearm). (Stop) Keeping your left foot in place, bring your right foot next to your left foot at point A into an informal stance facing B. Your eyes are focused straight ahead and both hands positioned in front of your waist as in the starting position.

31A

32

31B

31C

33

Stop

BAL-SECK

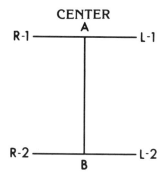

Ready
Stance

BAL-SECK

(Ready) Assume an informal stance at point A facing B, eyes focused straight ahead and hands raised in front of your chest, left palm wrapped around the right fist. (1A) Raise both heels and pivot your body to the left on your toes, simultaneously bringing both hands toward your left

1

Continued on next page

1B

shoulder. (1B) Leap a single step toward B into a right cross stance, simultaneously executing a right back fist strike to the face with your left palm placed on the outside edge of your right fist and forearm. (2A) Pivot 180 degrees to the left on the balls of your feet, sliding your left foot toward A into a left front stance. At the same time, execute an outside middle block with your left fist. (2B) Keeping both feet in place, execute an outside middle block with your right fist. (3A) Pivot 180 degrees to the right on the ball of your left foot, sliding your right foot toward B into a right front stance. At the same time, execute an inside middle block with your left fist. (3B) Keeping both feet in place, execute an outside middle

2B

2A

3A

3B

Continued on next page

4A

block with your right fist. (4A) Pivot 90 degrees to the right on the ball of your left foot, raising your right knee to waist level facing R. Simultaneously execute a low right hand block, palm up and elbow bent (the blocking surface is the inner edge of your forearm). (4B) Bring your right foot down toward R into a right front stance and simultaneously execute an inside middle block with your right fist. (4C) Keeping both feet in place, execute an outside middle block with your left fist. (5) Pivot 90 degrees to the left on the balls of your feet facing B in a horseback stance, simultaneously drawing your left fist over your right fist. (6) Keeping both feet in place, execute an outside knife hand block with your left hand, locking the

4C

4B

5

6

Continued on next page

7A

elbow (deliver the block in slow motion with tension). (7A) Keeping both feet in place, execute a right middle punch. (7B) Keeping your left foot in place, pivot to the left on the ball of your right foot (knee locked) and simultaneously execute an outside middle block with your right fist. (8A) Keeping your left foot in place, pivot back to the right into the horseback stance, simultaneously executing a left middle punch. (8B) Keeping your right foot in place, pivot to the right on the ball of your left foot (knee locked) and simultaneously execute an outside middle block with your left fist. (9) Pivot to the left on the ball of your left foot, sliding your right foot toward B into a right back stance, and simultaneously execute a middle knife hand block with your right hand.

8A

7B

8B

9

Continued on next page

10

(10) Pivot to the right on the ball of your right foot, sliding your left foot toward B into a left back stance and executing a middle knife hand block with your left hand. (11) Pivot to the left on the ball of your left foot and slide your right foot forward into a right back stance. Execute another knife hand block with your right hand. (12) Pivot to the right on the ball of your left foot and slide your right foot backward into a left back stance. Simultaneously execute a middle knife hand block with your left hand. (13) Pivot slightly to the left on the ball of your left foot, slide your right foot forward and behind your left foot in a left cross stance. At the same time, execute a high knife hand block with your right hand, left palm placed on the back of your right hand. (14A) Pivot 90 degrees to the left on the ball of your left foot, raising your right knee to waist level into a left crane stance, body facing L, face turned toward B. At the same time, bring both fists toward your left hip (left fist palm up, right fist palm in over

12

240

11

13

14A

Continued on next page

14B

your left fist). (14B) Execute a right side kick toward B and a right side punch (parallel to your kick). (15) Bring your right foot down toward B then pivot 180 degrees to the left into a left back stance facing A. Simultaneously execute a middle knife hand block with your left hand. (16) Pivot to the left on the ball of your left foot and slide your right foot forward into a right back stance, simultaneously executing a middle knife hand block with your right hand. (17A) Pivot to the right on the ball of your left foot, sliding your right foot backward next to your left foot in an informal stance facing A. At the same time, bring both fists down and to your sides. (17B&17C) Continue raising your

16

15

17A

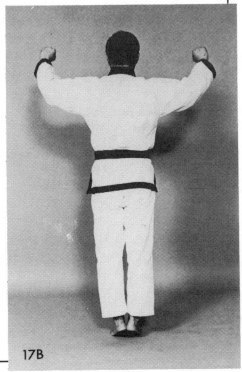

17B

Continued on next page

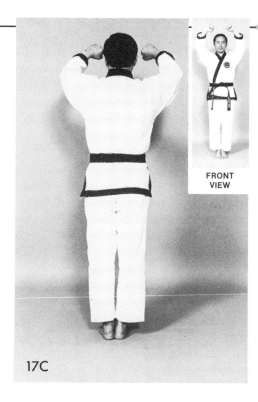

FRONT VIEW

17C

arms upward in an arc, executing a double overhead block. (18) Keeping your left foot in place, slide your right foot toward A into a right front stance, simultaneously executing a double hammer fist strike to the ribs. (19) Hop forward one step (sliding your left foot up to your right and then sliding your right foot forward) into a right front stance and simultaneously execute a right hand middle punch. (20A) Pivot 180 degrees to the left on the ball of your right foot and slide your left foot toward B into a left front stance. At the same time, execute a right spear hand strike to the midsection and draw your left palm toward your right shoulder. (20B) Keeping your left foot in place, pivot to the right on the ball of your right foot in a long left back stance. Simultaneously grab and pull with your right hand back and up until your right fist is behind your head, elbow bent at a 45-degree angle. At the same time, execute a low left

19

FRONT
VIEW

18

20A

20B

Continued on next page

21

block. (21) Keeping your right foot in place (and hands in same position), slide your left foot backward to your right foot into an informal stance, body facing R, face still turned toward B. (22A) Pivot 90 degrees to the left on the ball of your left foot and execute a right inside crescent kick toward B. (22B) Your left fist and right fist cross in front of your face to block. (22C) Bring your right foot down toward B into a horseback stance facing L. Simultaneously execute a low right hand block to the side. (23A&23B) Keeping both feet in place, turn your head 180 degrees to the left facing A and execute a left back hand strike at shoulder level.

22C

22A

22B

23A

FRONT
VIEW

Continued on next page

23B

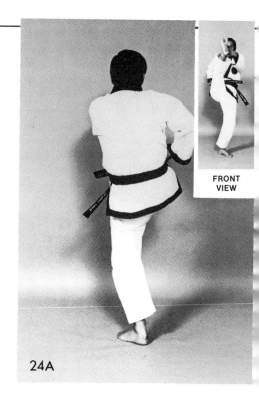

FRONT VIEW

(24A) Pivot 90 degrees to the left on the ball of your left foot and execute an inside (target) crescent kick toward A, striking your open left palm. (24B) Bring your right foot down toward A into a horseback stance facing R. At the same time, execute a right elbow target strike, hitting your open left palm. (25A) Keeping both feet in place, execute a low right hand block in front of your body, elbow bent, and tense your left fist at chest level, palm in. (25B) Keeping both feet in place, raise your right fist up and outside your left fist to chest level, palm in, and at the same time execute a low left hand block in front of your body, elbow bent. (25C) Keeping both feet in place, raise your left fist up and outside your right fist to chest level, palm in, and at the same time execute a low right hand block in front of your body, elbow bent. (25D) Keeping your left foot in place, slide your right foot toward A into a right back stance, simultaneously drawing both fists toward your left

24A

25B

24B

25A

25C

25D

Continued on next page

FRONT
VIEW

25E

hip. (25E) Pivot to the right on the ball of your left foot and slide your right foot forward into a right front stance, simultaneously executing a double punch toward A (left fist high, right fist low and palm up). (26) Slide your right foot backward next to your left foot into an informal stance facing A. At the same time, bring both fists toward your right hip. (27A) Execute a left inside crescent kick, hands held in position. (27B) Pivot 90 degrees to the right on the ball of your right foot, raising your left foot next to your right knee into a right crane stance (body faces L, your face still toward A). (27C) Pivot 90 degrees to the left on the ball of your right foot and step down toward A with your left foot into a left front stance. At the same time, execute a double hand punch (right fist high, left fist low and palm in). (28) Slide your left foot backward next to your right foot into an informal stance facing A. Simultaneously,

27B

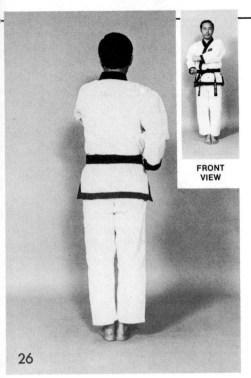

FRONT
VIEW

26

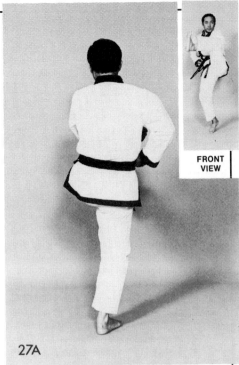

FRONT
VIEW

27A

27C

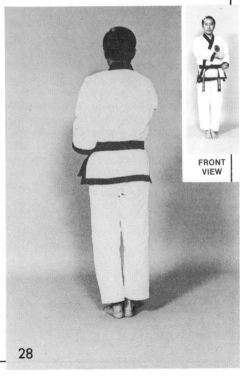

FRONT
VIEW

28

Continued on next page

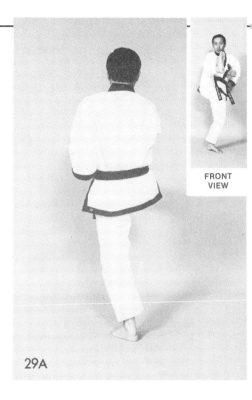

FRONT
VIEW

29A

draw both fists to your left hip. (29A)
Execute a right inside crescent kick,
hands held in position. (29B) Pivot 90
degrees to the left on the ball of your
left foot, raising your right foot next
to your left knee into a left crane
stance (your body faces R, face still
turned toward A). (29C) Pivot 90 degrees to the right on the ball of your
left foot and step down toward A with
your right foot into a right front
stance. At the same time, execute a
double punch (left fist high, right fist
low and palm up). (30A) Pivot 270 degrees to the left on the ball of your
right foot, sliding your left foot out in
an arc into a long front stance facing
L (right knee bent, leg parallel to the
floor), face turned toward B. Simultaneously execute a low right hand
block, palm up. (30B) Follow immediately with a right back fist strike
toward B. (31A) Pivot 180 degrees to
the right on the balls of both feet into
a right front stance facing R, left
knee bent, leg parallel to the floor. Simultaneously execute a low left hand

30A

29B

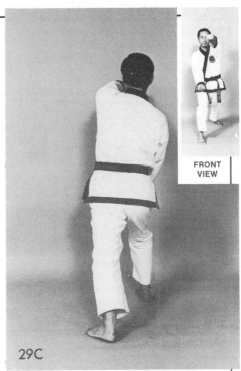

FRONT VIEW

29C

30B

31A

Continued on next page

block, palm up. (31B) Follow immediately with a left back fist strike toward B. (32) Pivot 90 degrees to the left on the ball of your left foot and slide your right foot toward B into a right back stance. Simultaneously execute a middle knife hand block with your right hand. (33) Pivot 90 degrees to the right on the ball of your left foot, sliding your right foot toward R into a right back stance. Simultaneously execute a middle knife hand block with your right hand. (34A) Keeping your left foot in place, slide your right foot backward toward B in front of your left foot. Simultaneously, prepare to deliver a left knife hand block. (34B) Slide your left foot a long step forward toward B into a left back stance (your right foot slides slightly forward as you enter the stance) and simultaneously execute a middle knife hand block with your left hand. (Stop) Pivot on the ball of your right foot and slide your left foot backward next to your right foot into an informal stance at point A facing B. Eyes and hands are the same as in the starting position.

31B

34A

32

33

34B

Stop